ENDO

This book has definitely felt like an answered prayer. It's so comforting to feel seen and heard and to know that you're not alone in what you're feeling or struggling with. Kelly brings hope by speaking of God's better way for us to live in His love and plan and by speaking of how He brought her out of her darkness. She is relatable, wise, and consistently humble and honest with her audience. I love how she incorporates science and behavioral therapy techniques into the process she went through and encourages in her book for healing from anxiety, but keeps God at the center of all of it. This book was such a blessing at just the right time!

—*Bianca Simpson*

Living Perfectly Loved has changed my life more than I ever expected. I was going through an extremely hard breakup, and I don't think I would have gotten back up on my feet the way I did without Kelly's book. It made me realize my worth, that God is in control, and that I was exactly where I was supposed to be in life. The lessons you will learn from this book are invaluable!

—*Haley Dickerson*

This book has given me the strength and tips to overcome my anxiety through the Word of God. Kelly's story of how she overcame her personal anxiety is inspirational and a must read!

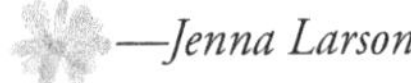
—*Jenna Larson*

Living Perfectly Loved has been such a blessing in my life. I have suffered from severe anxiety. This book is a testimony of Kelly's personal experience with anxiety and overcoming it, and that brings me such comfort. I feel like I'm understood and not alone. I would recommend this book to anyone for peace of mind and to help grow one's faith in God.

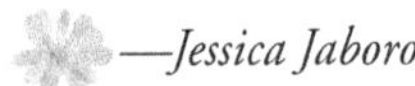
—*Jessica Jaboro*

Kelly's message was exactly what my heart needed when it was hurting and unsettled. This is an honest, genuine message from God that will provide more hope than you realized was possible. Anxiety can be paralyzing, but with the help of Kelly's book, anyone can overcome emotional distress. It was both encouraging and provided realistic steps to walk toward healing. Kelly's personal experience makes her message relatable, and she shows deep compassion for the hurting. This message will both test and strengthen you. It's more than a quick fix. Reading her book has pushed me to make the necessary changes that have allowed fulfillment to pour into my life in the way we all yearn for.

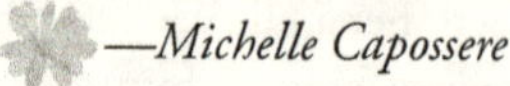

—Michelle Capossere

FOREWORD

We don't have to look far to see anxiety on people's faces. Recent statistics show that over 40 million people experience anxiety in the U.S. That's roughly 18.1 percent of the population. I will venture to guess that those numbers have increased since the start of the COVID-19 pandemic. As a therapist, my practice has been impacted daily with people who are experiencing stress, depression, and anxiety in increased numbers.

When clients come in and describe their symptoms of anxiety, I listen and offer this statement in response: "Anxiety distorts reality." It's like looking through a magnifying glass. Everything is bigger, more intense, and overwhelming. Indeed, we have lost our center.

It's in these fragments that anxiety fills in the empty spaces with *what if* and *oh, no*. Together, worry and anxiety have created a script that we recite over and over in our heads, something like, "This is too much, I can't handle it. It's going to be like this forever, and I'll never get over this." It plays over and over in our heads until we decide to change the script.

What you are about to read is a journey from fear and anxiety into a place of trust and peace. Kelly writes from a place of knowing the pain, battle, and defeat of crippling anxiety. It's real and relatable, and her journey is unique and universal. Change began for her when she realized she no longer wanted to continue thinking, believing, and behaving in ways that robbed her of experiencing the fullness of God's unconditional love.

Kelly's story of discovering hope in the midst of anxiety is both reflective and instructive. From her teaching background, she is able to give tools to the reader using Scripture in real-life examples. The 12-step approach she shares gives a guided process toward wholeness. Kelly describes her healing as a journey with starts and stops—and pauses to reflect, remind, and reframe her thinking using God's promises.

She weaves her experiences with faith, clinging to God's Word to help her climb out of the prison she felt trapped in. Hope emerges as she shares how she walked toward the light in the tunnel, step by step.

Living Perfectly Loved is a guide for those who feel hopeless and helpless in their struggle with anxiety. Kelly's story will offer encouragement, hope, and freedom as the reader engages in the process of believing God's promises for themselves. As she states in her book, her desire is for the reader "to feel equipped, encouraged, and inspired to continue on" in their quest toward healing and wholeness.

Pam Luschei
Licensed Marriage & Family Therapist
Author/Speaker

Living Perfectly LOVED

A Christian's 12-Step
Journey to Freedom from
the Grip of Anxiety and Fear

by

KELLY ANN SNYDER

Published by hope*books
2217 Matthews Township Pkwy
Suite D302
Matthews, NC 28105
www.hopebooks.com

hope*books is a division of hope*media
Printed in the United States of America by hope*books

First paperback edition.
Paperback ISBN: 979-8-89185-033-0
Hardcover ISBN: 979-8-89185-034-7
Ebook ISBN: 979-8-89185-035-4
Library of Congress Number: 2023951122

hb
hope*books

I dedicate this book to my husband, Todd, and
to my children, Riley and Janie—
May you live in the freedom Christ died
for all the days of your lives, and may His perfect love
always fill you to overflowing.

And for all those whose fear feels
greater than their faith—
May you dare to believe that freedom from fear is possible,
here and now, and may God's perfect love cast out every
fear that has threatened to keep you from
the freedom and fullness of life
promised you in Christ Jesus.

CONTENTS

There is no fear in love. But perfect love drives out fear, because fear has to do with punishment. The one who fears is not made perfect in love.

—1 John 4:18

INTRODUCTION: THE FATHER'S LOVE

There are many different fears people struggle with (and so many people are struggling with fear today). Fear of abandonment, fear of rejection, fear of failure, fear of intimacy, fear of death, fear of the future—just to name a few. Fear says, *I cannot trust God to keep me safe.* Fear says, *I must take control of my life.* Fear causes us to shrink back and hide, resulting in missed opportunities and unfulfilled God-given destinies. Fear causes anxiety, depression, increases our risk of developing health problems, and more. Fear is a liar! These issues are like heavy chains binding and oppressing those who have not yet come to understand the depth of their heavenly Father's love for them.

What began for me in 2011 as a desperate cry for deliverance from anxiety became a joyous, hope-filled journey deeper into the Father's open arms of love. During this time, God revealed to me that His perfect love had the power to cast out all fear, according to 1 John 4:18, which says, "There is no fear in love. But perfect love drives out fear, because fear has to do with punishment. The one who fears is not made perfect in love." Having struggled most of my life with generalized anxiety and fear, I suddenly realized that this one revelation from Scripture could completely transform my life and the lives of anyone who might also be struggling with anxiety and fear!

All fear—gone? The biblical truth that perfect love and fear cannot coexist both intrigued and baffled me. In one sense, realizing that God's perfect love had the power to free me from the hold anxiety and fear had on my life was liberating! But . . . I was already a believer. This caused me to wonder, *Could I be a believer in Jesus Christ, be saved for eternity by His loving sacrifice, and yet, not have the perfect love of God rooted and established in my life?* It became clear to me that I needed to understand more about what it meant to *live perfectly loved.*

Maybe right now you're struggling with feelings of hopelessness. You may feel completely overwhelmed by your life's circumstances. Maybe you doubt that you will ever experience freedom from the grip anxiety and fear have on you—but I am here to tell you that freedom is possible, here and now! You have a Father in heaven who loves you perfectly, and He is longing to take you on a journey deeper into His perfect love—where fear is rendered powerless, and you are free to become who He created you to be. He sees your pain. He knows the depth of your struggle, and He wants to meet you right in the middle of it—in the hardened, dark places of your heart that feel void of all hope, joy, and life and in the deep-down hidden places where shame, doubt, anxiety, and fear like to hide out. He will never leave you nor forsake you. He will see you through to victory!

However, there is only one way to the freedom found in the promise of His perfect love. Jesus said, "I am the way and the truth and the life. No one comes to the Father except through me" (John 14:6). Once, we were separated from the love of our heavenly Father because of our sin, but because of His great love for us, our heavenly Father made a way for us to be reconciled to Him—through belief in His Son, Jesus Christ! So this is where our journey out of living gripped by anxiety and fear toward *living perfectly loved* must begin—with Jesus!

The Bible tells us in John 3:16, "For God so loved the world that he gave his one and only Son, that whoever believes in him shall not perish but have eternal life." If you have yet to decide to make Jesus Christ the Lord and Savior of your life, maybe you are ready to take that step of faith now and to start your journey toward *living perfectly loved* with Him! If so, you don't have to wait. You can invite Jesus into your life by praying the following prayer out loud or in the quietness of your own heart:

> *Dear Jesus, I need You! I have made choices in my life that I regret. Sin has separated me from Your perfect love and the freedom You have wanted to give me. I want to start living my life for You now. I believe that You came to this earth to die on a cross to pay the penalty for all my sin, and for the sins of the whole world. I believe You rose again three days later and conquered death forever. Lord Jesus, please come into my life, forgive me for my sins, and make me the kind of person You want me to be. Help me to become so deeply rooted in Your perfect love that anxiety and fear can no longer have a hold on me. In Jesus' name I pray, Amen!*

If you just prayed to receive Jesus, all of Heaven is rejoicing with you now! You have just made the best decision you could ever make in life. Now you're ready to get started on your journey toward *living perfectly loved* as a new creation in Christ!

Whether you are just now beginning your relationship with Jesus or you have already been His follower for a long time, regardless of the degree to which you are currently struggling with anxiety and fear, I believe *Living Perfectly Loved* will serve as an encouragement and a support to you in your faith journey. This book is organized into three parts with a total of 12 chapters, and each chapter represents a different faith step you can take with the Lord to help you overcome anxiety and fear and grow in spiritual maturity.

In "The Rescue" (part one), I share the first five steps by which God began delivering me from the grip of anxiety and fear—steps that I believe God can use to deliver you too! Then, in "The Restoration" (part two), I share the four steps God used to begin healing my heart and mind from years of living in fear while simultaneously allowing my faith to be tested and strengthened so that I could become *strong, firm, and steadfast* in my faith in Christ (1 Peter 5:10)—steps that I pray will also help you develop unshakable faith. Lastly, in "The Release" (part three), I share the three steps God used to encourage me to look outside of myself and love others, to live out my purpose for His glory—steps that I believe will, in turn, repurpose your pain and complete the circle of healing God desires for you to experience from the effects of living gripped by anxiety and fear. It's been said that healed people heal people. I pray these three steps help you discover your kingdom calling to shine the light of God's perfect love and point others to Christ to bring glory to His name.

I wholeheartedly believe that each of these 12 steps will be a key for you to use to unlock the miracle God wants to work in you. While each step will build on the one before, keep in mind that everyone's journey is unique, and your progress will not be determined by how hard or how fast you work to get through to the end of the book—but rather by God's grace and perfect timing for you. Therefore, allow yourself the freedom to break between chapters (steps), if needed, to apply the message to your life. You may decide to circle back around to reread individual chapters you know you need to spend more time soaking in. This is especially important if you are keeping pace with a small group and need more time to process the information individually. Let God set the pace and lead you forward one small step at a time. Also, remember to be gentle with yourself and to give yourself time to grow. Healing is a marathon, not a sprint!

Finally, I want you to know that I've prayed for you! I've prayed according to the priestly blessing in Numbers 6:24–26—that the LORD would bless you and keep you along your way, that He would make His face shine upon you, be gracious to you, and grant you peace—in Jesus' name! I invite you now to journey through the pages ahead and discover how God wants to use these 12 steps of faith to free you from the grip of anxiety and fear so you can begin *living perfectly loved!*

PART I:
THE RESCUE

Some sat in darkness, in utter darkness, prisoners suffering in iron chains . . . Then they cried to the LORD in their trouble, and He saved them from their distress. He sent out his Word and healed them; He rescued them from the grave.

—Psalm 107:10, 19–20

STEP 1

CALL UPON THE LORD FOR HELP

I lift up my eyes to the mountains—
where does my help come from?
My help comes from the LORD, the
Maker of heaven and earth.

—Psalm 121:1–2

Alone, I sat in the darkness of my bedroom bearing a heaviness I could not shake. Anxiety tightly gripped my chest, and a dark cloud of depression loomed over me. *I know I can't give up,* I told myself. *But I can't keep going!* Rocking myself on the tattered carpet of my bedroom floor, tears streaming down my face, I was utterly desperate for an escape from the prison of my mind. The pain gouged so deep it felt almost more physical than emotional. I had reached my breaking point, and in my tormented state, I cried out into the darkness, "I just can't do this anymore . . . I want to die."

These thoughts came to me at my darkest time, when I couldn't see a way out of the prison of anxiety and fear I was in. Perhaps you've felt this way too. You've given it your all, but you've found it's not enough to free you from the grip anxiety and fear have on you. Believe me, I know the feelings of frustration, anguish, and hopelessness that come from struggling with anxiety and fear for so long. I know the tears you've cried because I've cried them too. I have felt the consistent tight grip on my chest that makes it hard to breathe freely, and I've nearly collapsed from complete exhaustion at the effort it takes to keep fighting anxiety day after day. I've experienced stabbing pain in the pit of my stomach—and the digestive upset that follows—whenever my fear is triggered.

I know the torment and debilitating pain caused by living with anxiety and fear—emotionally, spiritually, and physically. However, I can also say—because of how the Lord has since rescued me—I know the peace, healing, and freedom that is found in knowing and relying on God's unfailing, perfect love, and living in full surrender to His plans and purposes for my life. This is how I can say to you now, with confidence, that God has made a way for you to overcome anxiety and fear, hand in hand with Him. The question is: are you ready to take hold of God's hand now and begin your journey out of living in fear toward living perfectly loved?

My journey began in December, 2011. I didn't really want to take my own life, and I was sure I never would, but I didn't want to go on living life as it was either. I felt trapped in my pain, day in and day out, just trying to keep my head above water. Drowning in to-do lists and the responsibilities of being a wife, mother, and schoolteacher—tack on physical pain from a chronic health disorder—and it had all become too much! Most days, I didn't know whether to laugh deliriously in disbelief or drop to my knees and cry. This wasn't living. It was a daily fight for survival, and it seemed to me I was losing.

Perhaps you've experienced the kind of hopelessness I felt too, but your story is different from mine. Is your struggle with anxiety and fear related to the weight of responsibility you feel in your role as a wife, mom, and caretaker? Or maybe you work outside of the home, and you feel overwhelmed by the demands placed on your time and energy. Could it be that your anxiety and fear are trauma-related and the pain of your past is affecting your present? Maybe it's not your past but the future that you fear. Or maybe it's none of the above. Instead, it's that you've developed an acute phobia to something specific like speaking in public, flying on an airplane, germs, or being around crowds of people. Maybe you don't yet know the cause of your anxiety and fear. Whatever your personal trigger or cause is, though, one thing is for sure: anxiety and fear can affect us all to varying degrees—without respect to age, season of life, cultural influence, or professional experience.

I imagine you've tried all sorts of mind tricks to talk yourself out of being afraid and to stop the torment that anxiety and fear are causing you. In an attempt to stabilize my emotions and ground myself in hard reality when anxiety came to attack, I tried refocusing my mind on just the facts. The fact was: I was married to a hardworking, loving husband, and I was the mother of two beautiful children. The fact was: I was a tenured classroom teacher with the opportunity to positively impact the lives of many children every day. The fact was: I had friends and family that loved me. The fact was: I had eternal salvation in Jesus Christ! My life was not in shambles. Regardless of what my fearful feelings were screaming, I couldn't deny all the ways I was abundantly blessed. *So what was my problem really? Why the struggle?*

Feelings of guilt and unworthiness flooded me and made me feel selfish. Why wasn't I experiencing the joy of my salvation the way the Bible says I should? On the surface, everything in my life appeared to be just fine, but deep down, I was struggling with things I couldn't yet comprehend. I didn't see how those experiences affected my present, but God did. He could see the unprocessed pain and old wounds from childhood that had never healed properly. He could see the depths of my struggle with anxiety and fear and every dark, hidden thought and feeling I had let take root. He saw the holes in my heart, void of the love He longed to fill them with. He saw it all, and He loved me too much to let me stay where I was spiritually, lacking the fullness of life Christ died to give me.

The battle for joy and freedom had been long and fierce in my life. I had fought generalized anxiety and fear, along with bouts of depression, for as long as I could remember. I wrestled, wondering why I couldn't be like other Christians I knew, whose overflowing joy could be seen radiating off their glowing faces. They seemed genuinely happy and at peace. I longed for that kind of fulfillment. *Maybe that joy isn't for everyone,* I told myself. *Maybe I am supposed to struggle all the time. Jesus suffered for me. Why shouldn't I suffer for Him? This must be what picking up your cross and following Jesus daily looks like. One day, I will breathe my last, and the struggle will end. I will just have to endure until then.*

Like a teakettle coming to boil, whistling for attention, an internal alarm was sounding on that dark day in my bedroom when I hit rock bottom. *This is your wake-up call, Kelly!* I had reached a place in my spiritual journey where I knew God was calling me to start dealing with the deeply rooted sin in my life and the pain of my past. I could hear God saying, *Now is the time! I'm not going to let you put this off any longer.*

How had things gotten to the point that I no longer thought my life was worth living? The realization of just how bad things had become hit me, and deep down, I knew . . . *the only way I am going to get out of this pit of anxiety is with the Lord's help.* Right then and there, in the darkness of my bedroom, I got down on my hands and knees and cried out to God for help.

No, it wasn't the first time I had cried out to God in desperation. Maybe you can relate. You've cried out to God time and again, but it's as if your prayers have fallen on deaf ears. You wonder if God even hears you, if He cares. You think, *What's the point? Why keep asking God for help if He's not going to respond?* So, you stop asking God for help.

Here's what I can tell you: each time I cried out to God in the past and didn't receive the help I needed, it wasn't that God didn't hear me. It was that my pleas were for Him to do what I wanted done. I prayed, *God, take away my pain. God, stop anxiety from controlling my life, release me from its grip. God, stop these panic attacks from debilitating me any longer. God, remove these anxious thoughts from my mind and free me from the torment of all my worries and fears. God, take away this fear getting in the way of me living my life.* I had genuinely sought God for help through these prayers, but I hadn't been ready to put in the work and partner with God in my healing. I wanted God to wave a magic wand to take away the pain I felt and solve all my problems for me. I wasn't praying, *God, let Your will be done in my life.* I was praying, *God, let my will be done. I hadn't humbled myself or submitted to His will and His way of helping and healing me at all. This time, when I called upon the Lord for help, my prayers were coming from a place of true humility and surrender.*

Jesus said, "I have come into the world as a light, so that no one who believes in me should stay in darkness" (John 12:46). Jesus was with me when I could not find my own way out of the darkness. In my darkest hour, when I called upon His name, Jesus came to my rescue. His light broke through. My Savior was right there fighting for me—His light shining within me and all around me, commanding the darkness to flee. Jesus is with you now, too! He will lead you out of the darkness of living in fear and into the light of living perfectly loved in relationship with Him. It will take time, but by calling upon the Lord for help from a place of humility and surrender, you can begin the process with Him.

To get you started, I want you to be confident in two things. First, you are not alone. According to the Anxiety and Depression Association of America, "Anxiety disorders are the most common mental illness in the U.S." Anxiety is more common among women, as compared to men. "In addition, according to the World Health Organization (WHO), 1 in 13 globally suffers from anxiety. The WHO reports that anxiety disorders are the most common mental disorders worldwide."

So why are so many people struggling with anxiety these days? Perhaps the answer lies somewhere between the global pandemic and the increased isolation we've all experienced recently, our overcommitted schedules, an increasing number of broken homes, and the "need" for more, faster, bigger, and better of everything. Whatever the answer is, know that there are many people struggling with anxiety and fear today—you are certainly not alone!

In fact, the Bible contains many references to old heroes of the faith, such as the prophet Daniel, King David, and Elijah, who also struggled at times with anxiety and fear. Daniel stated, regarding a vision he had received from the Lord, "As for me, Daniel, my spirit within me was anxious, and the visions of my head alarmed me" (Daniel 7:15 ESV). David wrote in Psalm 94, "When anxiety was great within me, your consolation brought me joy" (Psalm 94:19). In 1 Kings, we read about a time when "Elijah was afraid and ran for his life" (1 Kings 19:3). The Bible says he went into the wilderness, sat under a broom bush, and prayed. "'I have had enough, LORD,' he said. 'Take my life; I am no better than my ancestors'" (1 Kings 19:4).

Oh, can I ever relate to how Elijah felt at that moment. What I love, though, is how the Lord responded to Elijah when he was overwhelmed with fear and had lost the will to live. The Bible says, "An angel touched him and said, 'Get up and eat'" (1 Kings 19:5). Miraculously, the Lord provided him with baked bread and a jar of water. Elijah ate, drank, and fell asleep. Then the angel came back and fed Elijah a second time to strengthen him for his journey to the mountain of God.

Like Daniel, David, and Elijah, we will have times where we will waver in our faith. When the *journey is too much* for us, we may forget all we know to be true about who God is and how faithful He's proven Himself time and again. We may lose sight of His perfect love for us and become afraid again. While they may have struggled with anxiety and fear, it's clear from Scripture that Daniel, David, and Elijah all knew to call upon the Lord for help in the midst of severe emotional distress. Yes, they struggled at times, but they were not held captive to fear.

Like the heroes of our faith, God also wants us to realize that when we need help, we can go to Him and trust that He will be with us to help us overcome all the powers of darkness that threaten to steal our peace. The Lord reassures us of this in His Word, saying, "So do not fear, for I am with you; do not be dismayed, for I am your God. I will strengthen you and help you; I will uphold you with my righteous right hand" (Isaiah 41:10). Friend, God will see you through this!

The second thing you can be confident in as you journey toward living perfectly loved is this: you do not have to live in fear. King David testified over and over in the Psalms how God rescued him from fear. He wrote, "I sought the LORD, and He answered me; He delivered me from all my fears" (Psalm 34:4) and "He lifted me out of the slimy pit, out of the mud and mire; He set my feet on a rock and gave me a firm place to stand" (Psalm 40:2). God doesn't play favorites. If He rescued King David from the miry pit of anxiety and fear, He will also rescue you.

God did not send His one and only Son, Jesus Christ, to live a sinless life and die on a cross so that you could remain a captive to anxiety and fear. You are promised complete victory in Jesus! Psalm 34:17 declares, "The righteous cry out, and the LORD hears them; he delivers them from all their troubles." We serve an amazing God who wants nothing more than for us to walk in complete freedom.

When the prophet Elijah needed the Lord's help, he knew where to turn. Rather than turn to idols or false gods, we know that he called upon the Lord for help. In 1 Kings 18:16–46, we read that the nation of Israel was waffling between faithfully worshiping the Lord and worshiping false gods. For many years, the prophets of Baal and Asherah had been leading the whole nation of Israel astray! The prophet Elijah was so grieved by their idolatry he sought help from the Lord on Israel's behalf. Led by the Spirit of the Lord, Elijah called for all the prophets of Baal and Asherah to meet him up on Mount Carmel. There, he erected two altars—one for the Lord and one for the false god, Baal. A bull sacrifice was placed upon each altar. Then, Elijah said to the people following Baal, "You call on the name of your god, and I will call on the name of the LORD. The god who answers by fire—he is God" (1 Kings 18:24).

Elijah was ready to settle the matter once and for all. Either the Israelites would choose to serve the one true God of heaven wholeheartedly, or they would serve Baal. The prophets of Baal cried out to their god to send fire down upon the altar they built and to burn up their sacrifice, but there was no answer. They continued throughout the day to call upon their god. Still, there was no answer. Then, Elijah called everyone over to the altar he had prepared for the Lord. There, Elijah called upon the Lord, praying, "Answer me, LORD, answer me, so these people will know that you, LORD, are God, and that you are turning their hearts back again" (1 Kings 18:37). The Lord sent fire down from heaven and completely burned up Elijah's sacrifice. Not only the sacrifice, but also all the wood and stones of the altar, the soil, and every lick of surrounding water that had been poured out over the sacrifice.

The Lord is faithful. The question we must ask ourselves is, will we trust Him to help us, or will we put our hope in the counterfeit gods of this world to save us? If we put our hope in false securities—like money, health, career, beauty, and other modern idols—we are guaranteed disappointing results. We will still be in need of salvation. If, instead, we put our hope in the Lord and call upon His name in our time of need, He will come to our rescue. While we can find relief from anxiety and fear in a variety of ways—some good and some not—our relief is typically only temporary and almost never complete. This is because there is only One who can truly save.

Our hope in Him will never be put to shame (see Psalm 25:3). God wants you to know that you can trust Him to show up in your time of need and help you. The Lord hears our prayers, and although the answers won't always look like what we expected, He "is able to do immeasurably more than all we ask or imagine, according to his power that is at work within us" (Ephesians 3:20). Just as the fire God sent down from heaven consumed not only the bull sacrifice but also the entire altar and everything surrounding it, the Lord will always exceed our expectations in response to our cries for mercy. As the Lord came down in power when the prophet Elijah called out to Him, so too will the Lord come for you!

> I lift up my eyes to the mountains—
> where does my help come from?
> My help comes from the LORD,
> the Maker of heaven and earth.
>
> He will not let your foot slip—
> He who watches over you will not slumber;
> indeed, he who watches over Israel
> will neither slumber nor sleep.
>
> The LORD watches over you—
> the LORD is your shade at your right hand;
> the sun will not harm you by day,
> nor the moon by night.
>
> The LORD will keep you from all harm—
> He will watch over your life;
> the LORD will watch over your coming and going
> both now and forevermore.
>
> —***PSALM 121***

Admitting I needed help was hard. It meant admitting I wasn't strong enough to fix my problem myself. To get the immediate help I needed, I had to first make the decision to relinquish pride and take up humility. The Bible tells us that from humility comes wisdom (see Proverbs 11:2). After crying out to God for help, He gave me the wisdom and strength I needed to know how to begin climbing out of the pit I was in.

This is what becoming humble and accepting the Lord's help looked like in my life. First, I opened up emotionally and let those closest to me in on how I was *really* doing. I listened to their wise counsel. Then, I contacted the counselor on staff at my church and made an appointment to meet with him. Having a professional set of ears to share my fears and feelings with, someone with years of experience, was very helpful in getting me started toward healing.

Next, I made an appointment with my primary care physician and carefully listened to the medical advice he had to offer. My doctor recommended keeping sugar and caffeine to a minimum, for example. Caffeine and sugar do not cause anxiety, but they will exacerbate anxiety symptoms. He told me to start exercising regularly, every day if possible. He also offered up the option of starting on anti-anxiety medication. Honestly, that piece of advice was the hardest to swallow, but with a deep gulp, I agreed to prayerfully consider it. It was a lot to digest, but I continued to put my hope in God, believing He would show me what to do next.

By God's grace, I was able to join two new classes at my church. One focused on developing a biblical self-image, taught by my dear friend and author Pam Luschei. The other class, taught by women's Bible study teacher Laura Banning, was on God's deliverance for His people from the book of Exodus. The timing of these classes couldn't have been more perfect for me. Alongside these two classes came the opportunity to join a couples' small group Bible study with my husband. Surrounding ourselves with fellow believers became a vital part of our spiritual growth, as a couple and as individuals. The amazing couples we were so blessed with, whom we now consider dear friends, were a source of constant support and encouragement to us both.

Right around the same time, I noticed in the church bulletin that the prayer team was meeting midweek. I started attending their meetings. Every week for several months, the faithful prayer warriors on the prayer team prayed for me, and God spoke healing words through them. I came heavy laden and left with my burdens lifted.

More opportunities continued to bud and blossom, producing an abundance of life-giving wisdom, healing, and blessings. I was in awe of how quickly God was moving to help me work through my struggle with anxiety and fear. My "ever-present help" (Psalm 46:1) was truly right by my side. As He gave me the strength to persevere through suffering, He added peace and joy to my character and filled me with hope. In and through all these opportunities for growth, God was working out His plan for my rescue, restoration, and release.

The journey to overcoming anxiety and fear is no easy stroll down a level street. It has physical, mental, and spiritual implications. The struggle is *real* and isn't the same for everyone. There are different causes, triggers, and degrees of severity. I do not know what triggers anxiety for you or what circles your brain may be running. I do not know whether anxiety hits you hardest in the morning or late at night, when you are alone or with other people, but I do know that God's perfect love is unchanging. He can be counted on to free you from every anxious thought and gripping fear you are now struggling with—no matter the source or cause. While your experiences and circumstances may be different from mine, you can be confident that as you grow in your understanding of God's perfect love for you, His love will fill you and drive fear right out of your life!

God has a plan. A plan to purify your heart, thereby removing anything that could separate your heart from truly knowing His. His plans are "to prosper you and not to harm you . . . to give you hope and a future" (Jeremiah 29:11). You can trust God with the process. Picture a child just learning to walk. The child's mother or father is there to cheer them on. They don't stand far away with their back to their child. No, they are within reach, face-to-face, excited, and ready to receive the child with outstretched arms. Yes, the parent knows their child might feel scared or nervous about taking their first independent steps. However, the wise parent also knows better than to take away their child's opportunity to learn and grow. They know their child needs to learn to walk. So they encourage their child to take their first steps, unsure as they may be, knowing that with practice their child will grow stronger and steadier.

Our heavenly Father is much the same. When you choose to take that first humbling step toward your heavenly Father, He will reassure you that He is right there, ready to embrace you in His loving arms. God will open doors of opportunity for you to walk through. It will be as though God is parting the clouds just for you—allowing His love and light to shine down upon you, thereby illuminating the path toward healing before you. God will reveal opportunities for growth and ways of gaining new knowledge and wisdom—but you will have to follow Him and take the necessary steps He calls you to, whether they be connecting with people you trust, investigating medical options, or looking into joining a small group at your church.

God is calling you to trust, to take your first steps on a journey toward living free from fear in His perfect love. You may feel unsure, but God knows what you can truly handle with Him. Jesus will be with you to guide you every step of the way, His Holy Spirit empowering you and encouraging you to keep putting one foot in front of the other. Some days you may take two steps forward and one step back or one step forward and two steps back. It's okay! God will be there to catch you should you start to fall or to pick you up and put you back on your feet those times that you do. He will not scold you for making mistakes. He will be there to cheer you on along the way until you finally arrive in His loving embrace, no longer anxious or afraid.

> In my distress I called to the LORD; I called out to my God. From his temple he heard my voice; my cry came to his ears.
>
> —*2 SAMUEL 22:7*

STEP 1:
CALL UPON THE LORD FOR HELP

STUDY GUIDE

1. How long have you been struggling with anxiety and fear? Can you recall when the struggle began?

2. Many who are struggling with anxiety and fear have been struggling so intensely or for so long they have given up hope of overcoming their problem. Do you believe *you* can be set free from anxiety? Now read Matthew 19:26. How does this scripture affect your answer, if at all?

3. Jesus said, "I have come into the world as a light, so that no one who believes in me should stay in darkness" (John 12:46). What does this verse mean to you? How can we move out of the darkness and into light?

4. Where, who, or what do you usually turn to for help? Do you feel these things are drawing you closer to God or pushing you farther away from His presence? Have you called upon the Lord for help?

5. What practical next step(s) do you sense God is calling you to take now? Make a commitment to taking one step forward this week.

6. Do you have a support network of at least three people who are willing to commit to praying, encouraging, and supporting you in your faith journey? If not, who can you make an effort to connect with in the next couple of days?

PRAYER:

Heavenly Father, Thank You for sending Your Son, Jesus, so that I do not have to remain in darkness but can live to enjoy the light of life. As I begin my journey out of the darkness and into the light of Your love, please take hold of my hand and remind me not to be afraid. Help me be humble and accept the help You offer in whatever form it comes. Draw me closer to You, show me Your deliverance, guide me in Your truth, and restore the joy of my salvation to me. All my hope is in You! In Jesus' name I pray, Amen.

STEP 2

UNCOVER EMOTIONAL TRIGGERS BY EXCAVATING YOUR PAST

Nothing in all creation is hidden from God's sight. Everything is uncovered and laid bare before the eyes of him to whom we must give account.

—*Hebrews 4:13*

After calling upon the Lord for help, your next step is to find out what's at the root of your anxiety and fear. One way our pasts creep into our present is through emotional triggers. Something we are experiencing in the present reminds us of something else painful we've experienced in the past, often causing us to feel fear and overreact in a big way. As you become more aware of your emotional triggers and when and why they exist, you will begin forming boundary lines around the distinct situations that are triggering anxiety and fear. Your problems will finally start making sense to you!

Once you realize lingering issues from the past are affecting your present, you can start excavating your past. When you commit to the process of excavating your past, the Lord will begin exposing the hidden places and dark lies that have kept you bound in fear. As scary as unearthing the pain of the past may be, it's a crucial step if you hope to experience deep inner healing and peace. So take a deep breath in, slowly exhale, and commit to doing the work of uncovering your emotional triggers by excavating your past. Friend, you're worth it!

Let's pray. *Heavenly Father, I'm ready. Open my eyes. Help me to see where this all began. How did I get here? Take me back to the places of wounding that didn't heal right and heal me. Whatever it takes, wherever You lead, I will follow You all the way. In Jesus' name I pray, Amen!*

Let me ask you this: Have you ever reacted so strongly in a situation that you surprised yourself with your reaction? Out of nowhere, you find yourself unable to control your emotions. Then, in the aftermath, you think, *wow, where did that reaction come from?* You recognize that you were overreacting, but you don't know why. Most likely, this situation was an emotional trigger for you. Emotional triggers are those situations, conversations, objects, sights, sounds, or other that trigger a strong emotional response out of proportion with reality or reason. When you are emotionally triggered, something about what you experience in the present reminds you of a painful past experience that you haven't fully processed and healed from.

Most people have emotional triggers. Emotional triggers work much like a learned response. For example, when I was a child, I unknowingly ate some bad tuna fish. I got really sick almost immediately. I was so sick that ever since that day, I have been unable to eat any kind of seafood. My past experience with tuna fish has dramatically impacted my present and future food choices. While that was a physical rather than emotional response, it follows the same pattern as emotionally traumatic experiences, which can significantly impact our long-term emotional well-being.

By becoming aware of your emotional triggers and when and why they exist, you will be able to begin forming boundary lines around the distinct situations that are actually triggering your anxiety. This will help you narrow the focus on your problem while widening your understanding of it. When you look, you will find there is a specific, concrete reason for every moment of strong emotion—fear or any other emotion—you experience. If you are someone who struggles with generalized anxiety, it's easy to see your struggle with anxiety as all-consuming, as if everything causes you anxiety in life. This is just not true, however. If you struggle with multiple fears or one fear that manifests itself in a variety of ways, the number of times a day you experience an episode of anxiety might be so frequent that you can't tell where one episode begins and another one ends. By taking the time to excavate your past, you will be better able to identify the root cause of your struggle with anxiety and fear. It will take time to trace each emotional trigger back to its root, but it is a critical step in overcoming anxiety and fear. Don't give up! It will come.

I had a lightbulb moment at the beginning of my quest for the root cause of my struggle with anxiety and fear. Every week, my small group Bible study leader asked this question: "Would anyone like to close us in prayer?" And every week, I dreaded it. Her request always made me feel so uncomfortable, as if I was being put on the spot. All of us in the group squirmed in our seats, wondering who would be the one to volunteer on our behalf. One week, I remember sitting in silence, waiting for someone else to agree to pray, when I heard a gentle voice within me say, *Speak up and pray for everyone. Say you'll do it!* It was the Holy Spirit urging me to volunteer to pray.

My heart began racing, my palms got sweaty, and I could feel my cheeks burning. Not only did I feel my normal insecurity about praying publicly, but now conviction was burdening my heart too. Still, I didn't open my mouth. I sat there stubbornly holding my breath, deliberately trying to avoid direct eye contact with anyone in the room. *What if I fumble over my words or, worse, forget to pray over someone's personal prayer request?*

After a long minute, a voice across from me interrupted my stream of thought. "I'll pray."

Whew! I was off the hook—or so I thought. The wave of temporary relief I felt quickly came crashing down into a sea of deep conviction. The uncomfortable silence had passed, true. But I failed to obey God's voice. I had missed an opportunity to allow God to speak through me and to bless my group—all because of my fear.

If you've ever participated in a church small group before, chances are you're familiar with the above scenario. Just to be clear, the conflict I felt was not because my leader was putting us on the spot to pray. The issue was my struggle with fear. All I needed was to stop being so concerned about what others thought of my ability to pray, quiet my soul, and simply speak to God. Instead, I gave into fear. I stayed silent. This was exactly what the enemy wanted.

This scenario repeated itself almost weekly, every time my small group met. It felt like too much—and my fear of praying publicly was just one of many fears I dealt with regularly! I realized it was time to stop the fear cycle and get to the bottom of what was triggering all my anxiety and fear.

Identifying small group prayers as an anxiety trigger was a jumping-off point—one of the first times I realized fear was controlling my life. It was also distinct, making it one of the easier triggers to begin unpacking. In excavating your past, it will take time to dig down deep and find the source of your pain. You will have to find a place to start digging like I did. Commit to the process of gaining wisdom and make an investment of time and energy. If you're like me, you will sometimes feel the process is taking longer than it should. You may dig down deep into your past—as far as you think you can possibly go—only to sense God saying, *Keep digging, you're not there yet.*

The truth is, God has been with you during every moment of your life, and He knows what experiences are still causing hurt in your heart. As children and adults, we often bury our pain, whether intentionally or unintentionally, vowing never to let it see the light of day. It may have happened so long ago that you have completely forgotten what you hid in the first place. Maybe you don't know what is causing such emotional distress; you only see the precarious emotional reactions, anxiety or other, that certain circumstances now provoke.

Rest assured, your exaggerated emotional reactions are not crazy. Your "crazy" has a place of origin. It's been trying to stay hidden. It does not want to be found out. You see, the enemy of your soul, the devil, is doing all that he can to confuse, shame, and distract you from seeing the truth. He wants to keep you from getting to the root of your pain because he knows that once uncovered, that suffocating weed can be uprooted from your life, and it will be unable to continue tormenting you.

God knows exactly where the root of your fear is hiding out, even if you don't yet. As you draw near to God and ask for His wisdom, He will reveal the hidden things to you (see Matthew 10:26), allowing you to walk in a level of freedom and closeness with Him you had only dreamed about. The Bible tells us, "Nothing in all creation is hidden from God's sight. Everything is uncovered and laid bare before the eyes of him to whom we must give account" (Hebrews 4:13).

Whether you're dealing with anxiety, fear, depression, anger, shame, unforgiveness, or any other deeply rooted issue, the Lord will point you in the right direction and show you where to start digging. "This is what the LORD says, he who made the earth, the LORD who formed it and established it—the LORD is his name: 'Call to me and I will answer you and tell you great and unsearchable things you do not know'" (Jeremiah 33:2–3).

King Solomon, the richest and wisest king who ever lived, recognized that wisdom was worth far more than riches. One night, the Lord appeared to Solomon in a dream and said, "Ask for whatever you want me to give you" (1 Kings 3:5). Of all the things Solomon could have asked for, he asked the Lord for a discerning heart. We, too, can ask God for this. In James 1:5, the Bible says, "If any of you lacks wisdom, you should ask God, who gives generously to all without finding fault, and it will be given to you."

The Lord gives wisdom to all who ask Him for it, but this wisdom does not always come easily. Don't let this discourage you! Instead, apply yourself to the task ahead. Pray for wisdom. Be patient but persistent. Seek the Lord and follow His lead. As the Bible says, we will have to seek wisdom like one might look for buried treasure:

> My son, if you accept my words and store up my commands within you, turning your ear to wisdom and applying your heart to understanding—indeed, if you call out for insight and cry aloud for understanding, and if you look for it as for silver and search for it as for hidden treasure, then you will understand the fear of the LORD and find the knowledge of God.
>
> ***—Proverbs 2:1–5***

Maybe you're thinking, *Why doesn't God just tell me what I need to know? Why do I have to hunt and search for the answers?* The thing is, God wants to draw you closer to Himself. If He just gave you all the answers, you wouldn't need to seek Him out. When we learn to seek God first, above all else, the answers will come, and the wisdom you gain from going through this process will be well worth the time and energy it will cost you. The Lord tells us, "The beginning of wisdom is this: Get wisdom. Though it costs all you have, get understanding" (Proverbs 4:7).

When Solomon so wisely asked God for a discerning heart with which to serve the Lord rather than fame or fortune, God not only granted his request, but He also gave him what he had not asked for—great wealth and honor. In our pursuit for wisdom and healing, may we not lose sight of what's most important—our relationship with the Lord!

Often a situation unravels so fast in the heat of the moment that we can't process it, and we don't take the time later to reflect on what happened to cause the problem in the first place. We may be so busy reacting that we have scarcely stopped to ask ourselves why we are reacting at all! It's after the heat of the moment has passed that we need to stop and find out the *why*—and that takes some digging. So, friend, take out your shovel, bucket, trowel, and brush, this is the time to start excavating your past!

As you get started uncovering emotional triggers, I suggest you keep a record of incidents in which you react strongly. Keep track of your emotional responses for a period of at least two weeks. I recommend getting a journal to record your thoughts, observations, findings, and the things you hear God speaking to you on this journey. You can also use the Emotional Triggers Log template provided for you in the back of this book or download the PDF from my website at kellyann-snyder.com.

Start by recording all the facts: who you were with, what you were doing, when it happened, where you were, and any physical symptoms you experienced. Record the thoughts you had right before and during the incident and specifically what strong emotions you were feeling. Also, write down whether the incident stirs up any memories from a painful past experience. After recording multiple incidents, look for patterns. Notice the similarities between the incidents. Going through this process will help you start pinpointing specific emotional triggers, when they happen, and why they occur. This can really be a helpful analysis of your ongoing struggle with fear or any other emotional response. As you work through the steps in this book, I encourage you to continue recording your triggers and responses. Keeping an ongoing record will not only help you be able to see the tremendous progress you will make over time, but it will also help you to remember God's faithfulness to rescue you from each and every fear.

Much of this process I have shared with you I've learned and adapted from a workbook called *Mind Over Mood* by Dennis Greenberger, PhD, and Christine A. Padesky, PhD. This is a secular workbook, first recommended to me by my Christian counselor at the time, which I found held many biblical principles. It gave me the perfect starting place to begin the excavation process in my own life, using a psychotherapy technique called cognitive behavioral therapy (CBT). This technique helps people to understand the relationship between their beliefs, thoughts, feelings, and subsequent behaviors. For this reason, I recommend getting this workbook or one similar. If nothing else, it may give you a place to start digging, like it did me.

When I began unearthing my past, I spent a couple of weeks recording in a journal all the situations in which I felt the most anxiety, fear, depression, and anger. After reflecting on them all, I was able to notice certain patterns of behavior. I discovered that I was constantly anxious when I had many tasks to complete. The longer my to-do list, the higher my anxiety level. Another one that probably comes as no surprise, given the story I just shared with you, was speaking in public. However, I also found that even in casual conversations with friends, I would get anxious. Job interviews were another big source of anxiety. My house not being clean or organized was overwhelmingly stressful. Getting dressed and ready in the morning was a consistently anxious time for me (and of course, it was part of my daily routine!). I felt depressed when

I thought someone was disappointed with me or anytime I felt I had let someone down. I became angry, even enraged, whenever I didn't feel listened to, acknowledged, or heard.

From the above situations, I dug into which ones were triggering the strongest emotional reactions from me on a regular basis, which I defined as once a week or more. One by one, I took the time to uncover what was at the root of each emotional response. I asked myself the following:

- What thoughts came to mind right before and during this situation?
- What was one strong emotion I was feeling?
- What is the first time I remember having this problem or feeling this way?
- What other times do I remember feeling this way?
- What time of day and how many times per day/week do I react this way?

I thought carefully about each one of these recurring issues and prayed to God for wisdom about where these strong emotional reactions stemmed from. I traced them back to other times in my past when I had felt the same way. Memories of the past came to me in images, words, and feelings. The Holy Spirit led me through those memories and helped me understand why they were now causing me to struggle in the present.

After identifying my triggers and excavating my past, the Holy Spirit revealed that all the fear I was experiencing pointed toward two core beliefs. These were subtle lies I was believing as truth: *I am not enough,* and *I am not loved.* These ideas were connected to each and every one of my fears causing anxiety. At the core of my being, I believed them as truth.

These lies were not independent from one another—they were interconnected. I would tell myself over and over again, *If I am not enough, I will not be loved.* I nursed this lie for years. I used many disappointing and painful life experiences as evidence to further substantiate these claims. My choice to believe these lies as truth, rather than the truth of God's unfailing love for me, opened the door for a fear of rejection and abandonment and a fear of man to become deeply rooted in my life.

What do you believe at the core of your being about God, yourself, and others? If you don't know, don't worry. God will help you uncover this and find the source of your pain. You'll know you've finished the excavation process when you've not only identified your emotional triggers, but also your core beliefs.

After uncovering your emotional triggers and excavating your past, it will be tempting to place blame on those people who caused you pain. You may want to blame your environment, your lack of resources, or any number of other factors.

I don't mean to minimize what happened to you; you may have been victimized, traumatized, or neglected in ways that were tragic and completely out of your control. Feelings of pain, grief, hurt, anger, and more are completely acceptable and justifiable in response to deep wounding. Processing emotions is both healthy and necessary! We get ourselves into trouble, though, when we allow places of deep wounding to fester. Festering wounds become fertile ground for resentment, bitterness, hate, and unforgiveness to take root in our lives. These are not only wrong responses, but they are also sin, and they will only lead to more pain.

This is called blame shifting, and its origins can be found all the way back in the book of Genesis. Since the beginning of time, that wicked serpent, the devil, has been bent on deceiving mankind, and mankind has struggled to resist his lies because of our sin nature. In Genesis 3, we read that Adam and Eve took and ate the forbidden fruit from the tree of knowledge in the Garden of Eden, thereby committing the first sin. Then when questioned by God, rather than own up to their sin, they were quick to shift the blame off themselves and onto someone else. Genesis 3:12–13 says, "The man said, 'The woman you put here with me—she gave me some fruit from the tree, and I ate it.' Then the LORD God said to the woman, 'What is this you have done?' The woman said, 'The serpent deceived me, and I ate.'"

Adam was quick to shift the blame onto his wife, and Eve was quick to shift the blame onto the serpent. While the serpent certainly deceived and tempted Adam and Eve to sin, both Adam and Eve were free to make their own choices and to later accept responsibility for their actions. Like Adam and Eve, when we do not take responsibility for our actions, we become blame-shifters.

While it's natural for us to want to point the finger at someone or something else in our pain, the most healing action we can take is to accept responsibility for *how we chose to respond* to what happened to us. None of us are immune to pain. In life, you will be hurt, and you will also cause hurt. We can choose to respond to the hurt in ways that either bring healing and peace or in ways that stir up more strife, anger, and pain. In other words, we become bitter or better.

One way we can respond well is to extend forgiveness to the people and situations that wounded us. Forgiveness is a choice, and one we can all make—even when we don't feel like it. Not in our own strength, but by the power of the Holy Spirit. If you make the conscious, willful choice to forgive, then the Holy Spirit will help your heart come around to it. In His power, you can forgive the person who is not sorry. You can forgive the person who refuses to change and continues to wrong you. You can forgive the person who doesn't deserve it.

None of us deserve forgiveness, but we are to forgive just as Christ Jesus forgave us (see Ephesians 4:32).

This does not mean that you need to allow ongoing, full access to your life to a person who has hurt you deeply and continues to do so unapologetically. You will likely need to establish strong relational boundaries with this individual to effectively guard your heart and avoid becoming their doormat. If maintaining a relationship with this individual is harmful to your physical, emotional, or spiritual well-being, you may need to consider whether it's time to let go of the relationship so you can move on with your life. We must pray for discernment in circumstances like these and seek wise counsel to know if and when we are to walk away, whether temporarily or permanently.

While reconciliation with certain individuals is not always possible, forgiveness is. Remember, Jesus didn't forgive us when we decided we were sorry, but while we were still sinners. Choosing to forgive is non-negotiable for the believer. The Bible says, "For if you forgive other people when they sin against you, your heavenly Father will also forgive you. But if you do not forgive others their sins, your Father will not forgive your sins" (Matthew 6:14–15). Forgiveness is the place where healing can begin. You will not experience healing without forgiveness, just as blame shifting will not produce the fruit of the Spirit: love, joy, peace, patience, kindness, goodness, faithfulness, gentleness, and self-control (Galatians 5:22–23). Blaming others for your choices only produces bitter fruit that will keep you in bondage, unable to heal from your past.

God wants you to see that He made a better way, through Jesus. It's time to start reprocessing our painful experiences in light of God's promises. Do you know that Jesus was with you in the pain that you experienced? Never did He leave you or forsake you. Can you picture Him there with you now? What do you think He wants to say to you? What would you tell yourself if you could go back in time?

Isaiah 53:4–5 says, "Surely he took up our pain and bore our suffering . . . He was pierced for our transgressions, he was crushed for our iniquities; the punishment that brought us peace was on him, and by his wounds we are healed."

I believe Jesus wants to say to you now: *Give Me your pain. Give Me your shame. Give Me your suffering and brokenness. Give Me your sin. I can take it. You don't have to carry the weight of it anymore. Your debt has been canceled. The debt you still feel owed by someone else because of the pain they caused you has been paid for with My blood. You can let it go. I died so that you can live!*

Your experiences, good or bad, impact the way you view yourself, others, and the world around you. Because our perception becomes our reality, the way we view our past experiences dictates how we respond to future situations. The reason for excavating your past, then, is not to relive the pain of the past or to throw yourself a pity party—although you may need to set aside some time to grieve your losses and talk with a friend, counselor, or pastor. It's not to discover the source of your pain only to start playing the blame game. The reason for looking into your past is to discover what lies you have believed that you need to surrender to God's truth, where you are in need of help and healing, and whom you need to forgive.

To heal, we need to ask God to uncover the deep places of wounding from our past and help us consider our responses. We need Him to help us understand how our emotional responses affected our actions and how our actions impacted us and those around us. Next, we need to take the time to pray and confess any sinful attitude that has taken root in our life as a result of the pain or trauma we experienced. Finally, we need to ask God to forgive us of our sins and help us heal. You may not have had control over what happened to you in the past, but you do have control over how you allow it to impact your present and future. Control what you can control and give the rest to God.

Jesus gives us hope. Look to Him to help you empty your cup of all the sin and pain from your past stealing from today's joy, and He will begin refilling your cup with good things with which to renew your spirit and satisfy your deepest longings. Jesus said, "But whoever drinks the water I give them will never thirst. Indeed, the water I give them will become in them a spring of water welling up to eternal life" (John 4:14).

If you are ready for real-life change and true healing, then forget everything you thought you knew about what happened to you. Listen for God's still, small voice and then move in the direction He wants to lead you. Excavate your past, exposing the dark lies and the hidden places that have kept you bound in fear. One by one, uncover the lies the enemy has fed you, that you have believed about yourself or others in response to your life experiences. Hold them up to the light of God's truth and watch as the darkness begins to flee. This will ultimately be a work of the Holy Spirit, but you will need to do your part and dig when and where He says to dig. Your labor of love, dedication to the process, and obedience will bring glory to God—and surely, He will deliver you.

The process I've described here of uncovering emotional triggers and excavating your past may sound simple, but I want to acknowledge that this is a complex problem, and there will be pain involved in confronting your past. You may even have an anxiety "flare-up." Meaning, you may notice an increase in anxiety symptoms temporarily as you work to get to the bottom of the root cause of your fear. My goal is not to cause you more pain, but only to point you to a starting place and offer some tools with which to begin your healing journey. Give yourself grace and time to peel back the layers of your life to discover the root cause of your struggle with anxiety and fear. This could take months or even years. Listen as God reveals truth about your life experience in His perfect timing. Wait on the Lord. Jesus will meet you at your place of wounding, and He will show you that He was there the whole time, and it was His perfect love that has carried you through.

I imagine Jesus looking deep into your eyes right now and saying, *I see your broken heart. The holes that were left by people you thought you could trust. I want you to know that I can fill those holes with My perfect love for you. I will repair the broken places. There have been times when you were not perfectly loved by others, but you need not fear. I will heal you with My perfect love. You can trust Me with your heart.*

> As for us, we have all of these great witnesses who encircle us like clouds. So we must let go of every wound that has pierced us and the sin we so easily fall into. Then we will be able to run life's marathon race with passion and determination, for the path has been already marked out before us. We look away from the natural realm and we focus our attention and expectation onto Jesus who birthed faith within us and who leads us forward into faith's perfection. His example is this: Because his heart was focused on the joy of knowing that you would be his, he endured the agony of the cross and conquered its humiliation, and now sits exalted at the right hand of the throne of God!
>
> ***—Hebrews 12:1–2 TPT***

STEP 2:
UNCOVER EMOTIONAL TRIGGERS BY EXCAVATING YOUR PAST

STUDY GUIDE

1. Do you sense there is pain buried in your past that needs to be excavated?

2. In what circumstances do you feel most anxious, fearful, depressed, angry, or other strong emotions? Describe one of your emotional triggers.

3. What past experiences might be pointing to the root cause of anxiety and fear in your life? Pray and ask God to reveal these to you.

4. Reread Matthew 6:14–15. Is God showing you someone now whom you need to forgive? If so, set aside time to do that as soon as possible.

5. Read Proverbs 4:7. Are you willing to commit to the excavation process? What sacrifices of personal time, energy, or other might you need to make in pursuit of a deeper relationship with your heavenly Father and God's wisdom?

6. Pray and ask God to reveal to you where you need to start digging. Consider keeping a record of your emotional triggers as described in the chapter (or using the Emotional Triggers Log in the back of the book or downloaded from my website) for a period of at least two weeks.

PRAYER:

Heavenly Father, I know that nothing is hidden from Your sight. You see the source of my pain, and You long to heal me. I acknowledge that true wisdom and understanding come from You. You are the wellspring of life! I want to understand why I have struggled so long with anxiety and fear and why I cannot seem to break free from the hold it has on my life. Lord, I ask You to reveal to me the places of wounding from my past. Guide me in Your truth, and lead me by the hand to wholeness and healing. In Jesus' name I pray, Amen.

STEP 3

TAKE CAPTIVE EVERY THOUGHT: FEAR IS A LIAR

We demolish arguments and every pretension that sets itself up against the knowledge of God, and we take captive every thought to make it obedient to Christ.

—2 Corinthians 10:5

STEP 3

I stared at the kitchen counter and sink stacked high with last night's dirty dishes. Peeking into the dishwasher, I breathed a heavy sigh. It was full of dirty dishes too! Quickly, I walked away to keep myself from becoming irritated by the mess, but there was no escaping my growing frustration. In the family room, the couch was piled with wrinkly but clean laundry that had to be sorted and put away. I gaped aghast, baffled by the sheer amount of clothing one family could cycle through in a week. Having just gotten home after a long day of work, I wasn't up for cleaning. What I needed was a place to sit down and put my feet up for a few minutes. So I headed to the TV room, desperate for some respite from the waiting chores. Big mistake. There were empty popcorn bowls and soda cans left from family movie night, throw blankets strewn about the sectional, shoes littering the floor, along with a couple of candy wrappers tucked between seat cushions. *Why doesn't anyone pick up after themselves?*

The day-to-day load of work and family responsibilities weighed heavily on me. It seemed there was never enough time to be present and simply enjoy life. I could feel the stress and overwhelm starting to rise from the pit of my stomach to grip my chest. Hot with anger and resentment, I stormed to my bedroom to lie down. I hoped to shut out all that didn't bring peace and spark joy when I closed my eyes, but it didn't work. I started to cry. *I can't do this anymore!*

Destructive thought patterns—such as *I can't do this anymore*, a phrase I used to tell myself regularly—attack our self-worth. They are abusive and oppressive, and they will attempt to destroy our identity in Christ. The next step after getting to the root cause of your struggle with anxiety and fear is taking a closer look at what current thought patterns keep you from breaking free from anxiety and fear. Fear is a liar! The truth is you don't have to let your thoughts take you captive.

To take captive means to take prisoner or to enslave. It's easy to get swept away by our thoughts and emotions and become a prisoner of our own minds, but you are not a prisoner. You have the power to "take captive every thought to make it obedient to Christ" (2 Corinthians 10:5). But what does this scripture mean by *take captive*? How do we make our thoughts *obedient to Christ?* It means that we replace thoughts that don't agree with the Word of God, who is Jesus Christ (John 1:1) or that contradict what He says to be true in Scripture.

I caught myself saying "I can't do this anymore" almost daily—in response to struggles at work, disagreements with my husband, an overwhelming to-do list, or the never-ending pile of dirty laundry and dishes. One day, I stopped and asked myself, *Is what I'm saying actually true? Can I not keep working, cleaning the house, and helping my family? Can I not work through disagreements with my husband? Can I not ease up on my to-do list and set more realistic goals for myself?* And most importantly of all: *What does God's Word have to say about all this?* I was starting to see how negatively this one simple phrase was impacting my outlook on life, my motivation for getting things done, and my commitment to my family.

After praying, reading my Bible, and learning the truth in Scripture, God revealed to me that the thought *I can't do this anymore* was actually a lie I was telling myself. The truth, according to God's Word, was that "I can do all things through him [Christ] who gives me strength" (Philippians 4:13). It hit me that this lie I was believing was holding me back! It had kept me feeling defeated rather than seeing myself as a conqueror in Christ. So right then and there, I made a decision. Instead of allowing that thought to continue deceiving me into believing something untrue about myself or about what God could do in and through me, I would replace it with the truth found in God's Word. Now whenever that old lie tries to creep back into my mind, I take it captive and make it obedient to Christ!

While this is just one example of how I started taking my thoughts captive and making them obedient to Christ, I use it to illustrate a point: God cares a lot about your thought life. Negative thoughts can lead to making false assumptions about ourselves, others, and God. They lead to drawing false conclusions about our circumstances. In choosing to believe our own thoughts and assumptions, as well as the lies the enemy whispers in our ear, over the truth of God's Word, what we're really saying is we don't believe God's Word to be true. If I say, "I can't," and God's Word says I can, then I'm acting as if God is a liar!

If, according to Scripture, "A good man brings good things out of the good stored up in him, and an evil man brings evil things out of the evil stored up in him" (Matthew 12:35), we need to be sure that we are filling our minds with and meditating on truths that reflect God's goodness and holiness. Whether we like it or not, good or bad, what's inside us will spill out onto others. My prayer is that what comes out of us may serve to benefit those around us and glorify God.

We have a choice—to believe our own thoughts and feelings or to believe God's Word. Friend, this is where your faith will be put to the test. Do you really believe what you say you believe? Have you let Scripture penetrate deep down into the recesses of your heart and mind and become deeply rooted? Will you trust God with your life?

Proverbs 3:5–6 instructs us, "Trust in the LORD with all your heart and lean not on your own understanding; in all your ways submit to him, and he will make your paths straight." The Lord will not lead you astray. You can trust Him. However, you must learn to fully receive God's Word as truth if you want to grow in faith.

If anxiety and fear have a grip on you, then somewhere along the way you've allowed fearful thoughts and feelings to take control of your mind rather than God's truth. The good news is you can regain control of your mind. 2 Timothy 1:7 says, "For God gave us a spirit not of fear but of power and love and self-control" (ESV). If you sense that you are making decisions based on what a spirit of fear is whispering instead of what God's Word has told you is true, please do not let this shame you in any way. Rather, let it shine a light on the dark places in your heart and mind yet to be surrendered to the Lord. Let it open your eyes to the schemes the enemy has devised to keep you from the freedom and fullness of life promised you in Jesus Christ.

We are not subject to our own thoughts because "we have the mind of Christ" (1 Corinthians 2:16). With the sword of the Spirit, which is God's Word (Ephesians 6:17)—and the power of the Holy Spirit within us—we can overcome every lie the enemy could use to tear us apart. If possible, stop and pray right now, asking the Lord to show you at least one Bible verse this week that you can use to break free from a lie you've been believing. Once God shows you the verse, make it your go-to verse whenever that lie tries to creep back into your mind and you are tempted to believe it.

Consider framing Scripture and hanging it up in your home. Make a point to memorize Scripture and declare it out loud whenever you feel overwhelmed by anxiety and fear. Keep Scripture close at hand, maybe in your purse, back pocket, or cell phone. This is your best offense against the attacks of the devil.

The Word of God is your sword in hand with which to pierce the enemy's lies. It's a source of light in a dark moment. Use it as a weapon in your fight for freedom. If you need help getting a jump start on this, I've provided "A Guide to Taking Captive Every Thought" in the back of this book. It contains some of the most common lies we fall for, along with two truths from Scripture to replace each lie with.

When we take time to study and meditate on the Word of God, the distinction between His Holy Word and our own thoughts will become more and more clear. It's like comparing apples to footballs. There is no comparison! God declares, "For my thoughts are not your thoughts, neither are your ways my ways" (Isaiah 55:8). If we want to be victorious over our enemy and know the truth, we must seek out wisdom and understanding from God's Word. Know God, know truth. No God, no truth. That's how it works!

God tells us in His Word what He wants us to fill our minds with: "Finally, brothers and sisters, whatever is true, whatever is noble, whatever is right, whatever is pure, whatever is lovely, whatever is admirable—if anything is excellent or praiseworthy—think about such things" (Philippians 4:8).

This is our recipe for success! When we think about only these things, there is no room left for anything that may cause anxiety or fear and hinder our walk with God. If you are unsure whether your thoughts are in line with God's Word, I recommend running it through the litmus test of Philippians 4:8. Anything that does not pass this test is something you should not be thinking about or agreeing with!

When you feel anxious, fearful, discouraged, confused, stuck in a bad mood, or when your day isn't going in the direction you'd hoped, and you need God to turn things around, it's time to pray! One prayer I often pray is: "Lord, transform me by the renewing of my mind" (taken from Romans 12:2).

Praying this prayer helps me hear God's voice more clearly and see things from His point of view. Asking God to renew my mind opens the door for Him to help me out of the wrong attitude or thought process I'm stuck in. I ask Him to show me His Word for the moment. I ask Jesus to intercede on my behalf, and to reestablish me in His perfect peace. It works every time!

Have you ever stopped to consider that some of the thoughts running through your head might not be your own? I don't mean to say you're hearing voices—at least not in the way that would make you want to question your sanity. I simply mean that our thoughts can be spoken by different voices: the voice of God, our own internal voice, and even the voice of the enemy. The Bible warns us: "Dear friends, do not believe every spirit, but test the spirits to see whether they are from God, because many false prophets have gone out into the world" (1 John 4:1).

Picture with me a confused, forlorn-looking character, with a devil standing on one shoulder, and an angel standing on the other. George Bailey, the main character in the classic Christmas movie *It's a Wonderful Life,* is who first comes to mind. Maybe you've seen this movie, or a similar scene in another movie or cartoon show, and know how this scene plays out. The confused character listens to what both the angel and the devil have to say, turning his head from one shoulder to the other. What the devil says appeals mostly to the character's fleshly desires for greed, lust, or pride, but what he says is also manipulative in that it plays on the character's weaknesses, insecurities, and fears. What the angel says seems to resonate with what the character knows deep down to be true and the right thing to do, but often this advice is harder to initially follow, either because it's less appealing or the character has lingering doubts about whether they will truly benefit from following the angel's advice.

In other words, do not trust every voice—whether it's coming from inside your own head or even from your best friend. Be discerning when choosing whose advice to take and what thoughts you will give power to. Stay alert to the devil's schemes and decide to submit only to the voice of the Holy Spirit. God does not want you to be deceived! It may be that your own thoughts aren't lining up with God's Word or that your well-meaning friend doesn't quite understand God's will for a particular circumstance. Some people can be very trusting of authority figures, especially Christian ones, but we also need to test their lessons against Bible truth, especially now. You may be hearing the voice of the Holy Spirit leading you down the path of righteousness, or the enemy may be trying to deceive you. Take every thought captive; hold it up to the light of God's Word. If a thought doesn't align with what the Bible says, that thought needs to go.

While we won't actually see a devil or an angel sitting on our shoulders, we will feel the alluring pull of what the devil says and be tempted to believe him over the truth of God's Word. So how do we combat the voice of the enemy? Make the switch and replace ungodly thoughts with Scripture. The Bible tells us, "Submit yourselves, then, to God. Resist the devil, and he will flee from you" (James 4:7). When the enemy comes to attack, I find it helps me to declare God's Word out loud. When you declare something out loud, it's as if you're taking a firm, authoritative stance. I want to be sure the enemy hears me loud and clear: *I'm resisting your lies, and you have no authority against what God's Word holds to be true!*

There is power in declaring God's Word out loud. Satan is not God. He can't read our minds, and he is not omniscient. However, he can hear our voices. I might say something like:

"No, Satan, it is a lie that I'll never overcome anxiety, because God's Word says, 'everyone born of God overcomes the world' (1 John 5:4). You must flee from me now, Satan, in the name of Jesus!"

What about God's voice? How can we know for certain we are hearing God's voice versus our own voice or the voice of the enemy? Personally, my confidence has grown in discriminating between these voices over time through regularly drawing close to God in prayer, consistently reading my Bible, and being intentional with taking my thoughts captive and making them obedient to Christ. However, if I find myself still questioning my ability to discern, I make a point to seek out other believers in Christ whose wisdom and walk with God I deeply respect to get their feedback. I find God often confirming a thought or idea I've had was from Him by speaking to me through other believers (see 1 Chronicles 16:15–17 and Job 28:27–28). God's Word tells us, "My sheep listen to my voice; I know them, and they follow me" (John 10:27). It may take some time for you to learn to recognize the way God speaks to you, but if you have invited Jesus to come into your life to be your Lord and Savior, then He is your Shepherd, and you *will* hear His voice.

I think many of us tend to experience something similar to Samuel when we're learning to recognize the voice of God. The first time the Lord called Samuel, he heard someone call to him, but he did not recognize the voice of the one calling.

> Then the Lord called Samuel. Samuel answered, "Here I am." And he ran to Eli and said, "Here I am; you called me." But Eli said, "I did not call; go back and lie down." So he went and lay down. Again the Lord called, "Samuel!" And Samuel got up and went to Eli and said, "Here I am; you called me." "My son," Eli

> said, "I did not call; go back and lie down." Now Samuel did not yet know the LORD: The word of the LORD had not yet been revealed to him. A third time the LORD called, "Samuel!" And Samuel got up and went to Eli and said, "Here I am; you called me." Then Eli realized that the LORD was calling the boy. So Eli told Samuel, "Go and lie down, and if he calls you, say, 'Speak, LORD, for your servant is listening.'" So Samuel went and lay down in his place. The LORD came and stood there, calling as at the other times, "Samuel! Samuel!" Then Samuel said, "Speak, for your servant is listening."
>
> ***—1 Samuel 3:4–10***

Samuel didn't recognize the Lord's voice at first because he had never heard it before, and the Word of the Lord had not yet been revealed to him. Even though Samuel had been serving the Lord in the temple almost his whole life, he still did not know the voice of the Lord. Similarly, maybe you've been a Christian for a long time, but you have never really heard God speaking to you.

God may speak to us through our consciences, other people, dreams and visions, and countless other creative ways, but mainly God speaks to us through His Word. God's Word is revealed to us through the power of the Holy Spirit when we read or listen to our Bibles, through books or other sources containing Scripture, through pastors, etc. The more we read, listen to, and meditate on God's Word, the easier it will be for us to recognize God's voice when He is speaking to us.

The Bible is literally the Word of God. When we talk about the Word of God, we aren't merely referring to the message in the Bible; the Word of God is also the living person of Jesus. John 1:1 says, "In the beginning was the Word, and the Word was with God, and the Word was God." Since Jesus is the

Word made flesh (see John 1:14), and His Spirit who dwells in us gives us life (see Romans 8:11), we can conclude that the Word is life. If you want to have a full life, get filled up with the Word of God! Jesus is also the light of the world (see John 8:12). Therefore, the Word is light. It is "a lamp for [our] feet and a light on [our] path" (Psalm 119:105). If we follow the light, God promises we will never walk in darkness. The Word gives us victory over the powers of darkness (see Ephesians 6:11–13), victory over our sin (see 1 Corinthians 15:56–57), and authority to crush the head of the serpent (see Genesis 3:15). Jesus is truth. He told His disciples, "I am the Way and the Truth and the Life" (John 14:6). Thus, the Word is truth (see John 17:17). "Know the truth," Jesus said, "and the truth will set you free." (John 8:32). Finally, "all Scripture is God-breathed" (2 Timothy 3:16). Breathe it in! Inhale truth, hope, joy, peace, and love. Exhale shame, doubt, struggle, pain, and fear. Breath of life breathe on us!

When I started seeking the Lord wholeheartedly and diving into His Word, the Bible came alive to me for the first time. I will admit that I used to struggle with not falling asleep reading the Bible, but now I hang on every word because I know it is the very Word of God spoken to me. Oftentimes, the Holy Spirit will prompt me to notice particular verses. It's as if the words are jumping off the page at me! I sometimes recall a verse in the middle of a conversation with someone, which might be God prompting me to share it with that person to encourage them. When I see or hear a particular verse repeatedly in a short period of time from different sources, I know God is speaking to me, asking me to pay attention and understand something.

My advice to you is this: be obedient to reading His Word daily—even when you don't feel like it—and the Holy Spirit will help you understand it and thereby recognize God's voice.

It will come like rushing water, flowing from the heart of God straight to you. He will write His Word on your heart. His Word will begin to flow through you too!

If we do not listen and believe the Word of God, we will remain easily swayed by the lies fear speaks to us. Some fearful thoughts and reactions may even become so deeply ingrained within us that they become *automatic thoughts* and *physiological responses.*

Automatic thoughts are thoughts that sweep through your mind without you even consciously thinking about them. According to the *American Psychological Association (APA) Dictionary*, "They have been so well learned and habitually repeated that they occur without cognitive effort." They can be so subtle that if you aren't paying attention, you may carelessly let them through the front door of your mind without first considering whether you want to invite them in and entertain them. Adopting them as your own voice doesn't happen overnight either, but is usually the result of years of conditioning.

Automatic thoughts generated in response to threatening or otherwise stressful situations can lead to what is known as a "fight-or-flight" response. A fight-or-flight response, first described by Walter B. Cannon, is defined by the American Psychological Association (APA) as "a pattern of physiological changes elicited by the sympathetic nervous system." According to this APA definition, "Specific sympathetic nervous system responses involved in the response include increased heart rate, respiratory rate, sweat gland activity, elevated blood pressure, decreased digestive activity, pupil dilation, and a routing of blood flow to skeletal muscles. In some theories, such changes are the basis of all human emotions." Meaning, your brain has literally been wired to register certain situations or stimuli as threatening or dangerous, causing you to physically respond in fear before you even have time to think.

If your brain has determined that what you are experiencing is something to fear, your heart may start pounding, your palms may get sweaty, your stomach may do flip-flops or start cramping, your muscles may tighten, you may have trouble concentrating, and your breathing may become shallow—among other symptoms. If anxiety has become a lifestyle, and fight-or-flight is your typical response, you're at risk of causing undue stress on your nervous system. Your body wasn't made to handle ongoing high levels of stress. Stress is well known for causing disastrous effects on our bodies. In fact, autoimmune diseases can sometimes be attributed to chronic anxiety and long-term stress. I share this not to scare you but to drive home the point that if you aren't intentional with the thoughts you allow yourself to think, you can become easily trapped in destructive thought patterns that will keep you from recognizing God's voice and truth for you.

If you look at the Emotional Triggers Log I mentioned in Step 2, you may notice that there is space to record your thoughts. Part of understanding your emotional triggers is beginning to recognize the thoughts you have surrounding them. If you attempted the Emotional Triggers Log and found it difficult to record your thoughts just before a trigger, it may be because these thoughts have become subconscious. Meaning: you're barely aware of them, they pop into your head without your permission, or they're feelings that don't fully register into words. If so, try to start paying extra close attention to your thoughts the next time anxiety is triggered and write down what you think about as soon as possible. Writing down your thoughts and fears is one way to begin taking captive every thought and making them obedient to Christ.

When I went through this process, I took a long hard look at my list of recorded thoughts and carefully considered what I was allowing myself to think and believe. Until taking time to do this, I didn't realize just how negative and off-base many of my thoughts were. I started to see just how hard I had been on myself—how condemning and abusive my thoughts were. The enemy wanted me to believe that there was no hope of a more abundant life for me and that I might as well give up. He wanted me to believe that I could never overcome all my fear. He wanted me to believe that I was not enough. He wanted me to believe that I was unloved.

These lies had tried to stay hidden, but by writing them down, I was systematically identifying and boldly calling out each one. Then, taking each thought captive one by one, I declared the truth of God's Word, thereby commanding my thoughts to become obedient to Christ. My old, dead way of thinking got the boot. I made room for God's truth in my thought life, and I let His Word transform me. The darkness began to flee, and the light of Jesus grew brighter within me. Anxiety and fear dissipated, and the perfect love of Jesus took their place. I'm telling you, friend, learning to take captive every thought and make it obedient to Christ was a game changer!

What does your internal dialogue sound like? Begin writing down the thoughts you hear yourself say in your journal and work on becoming more conscious of your inner dialogue. As you learn to recognize and recall your thoughts, ask yourself, *What thoughts hold true when held up to the light of God's Word, and which thoughts turn to ash when tested with His holy fire?* Pay particular attention to the thoughts you have during times of high anxiety, anger, depression, or other strong emotions. What are you telling yourself? What thoughts are you giving power to? You may be surprised to discover how many lies you have agreed with.

The truth is we struggle to believe God's Word because the pain of our past experiences seems to confirm that our darkest thoughts and worst fears will come true. We all too often believe the lie over what's true because our memories seem more real than the possibility of a positive outcome, safety, and peace. But when we trust in the past, we forget who holds our future in His hands. In fear, we try to prepare ourselves for the worst possible outcomes, but our past doesn't determine our future, and neither do our present circumstances. Fear is a liar! Don't listen to its lies! Listen to the voice of the One who created you in His image, who calls you chosen, and declares that you are His: "'For I know the plans I have for you,' declares the LORD, 'plans to prosper you and not to harm you, plans to give you hope and a future'" (Jeremiah 29:11).

God's Word is true, all the time. It's true even when we don't understand it or believe it. It's not a subjective truth based on individual circumstances, but it is objectively true for all people. Maybe you think, *But I'm different. You don't know my situation.*

It takes faith to believe that what God says is true. You can ask God for the faith to believe (see Mark 9:23–24). Ask God to reveal His Word to you and cling to it. And when you can't distinguish the lies from the truth, make God's Word your only truth. Let His Word transform your mind and give you peace. The Bible promises, "For no word from God will ever fail" (Luke 1:37).

Do you know our heavenly Father loves you and will stop at nothing to get to you? He is fiercely and passionately pursuing you, throwing the lies out of the way so He can come and rescue you! Can you even begin to comprehend the depth of God's perfect love for you? God tells us He loves us, but if we don't believe it, we will not be able to receive it. If we don't allow God's Word to reside deep within our hearts, we will never know the depth of His perfect love for us—or experience true freedom from fear. This is such an important concept to grasp.

Please hear me on this: you do have control over your thought life, and the choices you make can either keep you stuck in fear or allow you to experience God's love and true freedom. God is not withholding His love from you. He's holding it out to you! Will you open your heart and mind to accept it? You can decide right now to start taking every thought captive and making them obedient to Christ. You don't have to settle for anything less than living perfectly loved!

> Blessed is the one who does not walk in step with the wicked or stand in the way that sinners take or sit in the company of mockers, but whose delight is in the law of the LORD, and who meditates on his law day and night. That person is like a tree planted by streams of water, which yields its fruit in season and whose leaf does not wither—whatever they do prospers.
>
> —***Psalm 1:1–3***

STEP 3:
TAKE CAPTIVE EVERY THOUGHT

STUDY GUIDE

1. What does your internal dialogue sound like? Think about phrases you regularly tell yourself and write them down. What is your overall impression of your self-talk? What thoughts are you giving power to?

2. How is your internal dialogue impacting your emotions and subsequent choices? Does it encourage you to step out and try new things, or does it make you fearful and timid? Does it lift you up and strengthen you, or does it bring you down? Does it bring you closer to other people, or is it isolating? Does it lead you to want to say *I can* or *I can't?*

3. God tells us what He wants us to think about. Take one of the thoughts you wrote down in answer to question number one and run it through the filter of Philippians 4:8. Does it adhere to the guidelines God provides us within this verse? If not, how can you now take that thought captive and make it obedient to Christ? (See "A Guide to Taking Captive Every Thought: Replacing Worn-Out Lies with God's Truth" in the back of the book for help with this.)

4. What Bible verses do you have close at hand with which to resist the enemy? Try to build up knowledge of five to ten go-to verses that you can quickly reference in a moment of need. Identify at least three verses now and begin memorizing them.

5. Are you still feeling stuck, in need of a mental reset? Try praying Romans 12:2, "Lord, transform me by the renewing of my mind." Ask God to help you see things from His point of view.

PRAYER:

Heavenly Father, I confess it's often hard to distinguish my thoughts from Your thoughts and the lies of the enemy from the truth of Your Word. Lord, make Your Word my only truth. Begin revealing Your Word to me in greater measure. Help me to recognize Your voice. Grow in me a desire to seek You in Your Word, and through Your Word, give me the wisdom and power to overcome my every fear. In Jesus' name I pray, Amen.

STEP 4

SURRENDER YOUR LIFE AND LIVE FOR CHRIST

Whoever wants to be my disciple
must deny themselves and take up
their cross daily and follow me.
For whoever wants to save their life
will lose it, but whoever loses their
life for me will save it.

—Luke 9:23–24

God uses times of testing to reveal to us what we have yet to surrender to Him. Learning to surrender the things we are holding on to so tightly is part of relying on God alone for our every need. We must shift our focus from the temporary things of this world to eternity. Once you've called upon the Lord for help, excavated your past, and taken captive every thought, you are ready to take the next step in your journey toward living perfectly loved—to live for Christ in total surrender.

Total surrender happens when our fleshly desire, or human will, is broken. When we finally come to the end of ourselves, our hearts, minds, and bodies are ready to fully submit to God's will and to live for God's glory instead of our own pleasure or ideals. To be completely honest, this is where many choose to turn around and walk the other way. It can be difficult to abandon control over our own lives, especially when we have struggled for so long over uncontrollable fear. There are many who aren't ready to give up living life on their terms. They count the cost and say, *It's too much!* Before you count the cost as too high, let me encourage you: only if you die to yourself and live for Christ will you find true freedom, purpose, and fullness of life.

Let me tell you about one of the first times I had to surrender my spirit of fear to God and live within His freedom. As my family and I were driving home from church one Sunday, my son, Riley, excitedly asked my husband and me, "Can we go to Indian Hills summer camp this year?"

My daughter, Janie, piped in, "We saw a video of the camp and all things that we can do there! You get to sleep in covered wagons and play in a tree house!"

They handed me the flier with all the details. It would be four days and four nights. I wanted to share in my children's enthusiasm, but instead, my mind instantly began filling with anxious thoughts and *what-if* questions. *Can the camp counselors and staff be trusted?* My son has life-threatening food allergies to wheat and peanuts. *Will the camp be able to make accommodations for his dietary needs and ensure his safety?* My daughter has Snow White's complexion. In the extreme heat of summer, I wondered, *Who will make sure she is properly covered with sunscreen all throughout the day?*

The idea of sending my babies away to an overnight camp for the first time made my stomach churn. *Second and third grade is too young to go away overnight,* I told myself. I had just made up my mind that camp was out of the question when I felt the Holy Spirit nudging me to reconsider. I sensed that God had plans and reasons I didn't yet understand for them to attend camp. It seemed God was calling me to surrender to Him my fears about my children's safety, to release control, and to trust that He would look after my children while they were away.

My husband and I talked it over that afternoon, and we finally agreed we would let them go. However, there was still the question of cost. How much was this blessed camp going to run us anyway? Quickly adding up the cost in my head, I carelessly blurted out the total amount in front of both kids. "Yikes, $700!" *Oops,* I thought. I hadn't intended to lay a burden of guilt on my kids for wanting to go to church camp.

Looking inspired, Riley ran off to his bedroom, returning seconds later with his wallet in hand. Opening it up, he pulled out his cash and handed me the entire sum: $130. This was all the allowance and birthday gift money he had been saving for over a year. For a kid without a job, this was a lot of money! "I want you to have it to help with the cost of camp," he said.

I stared at him dumbfounded, not quite knowing how to respond to such incredible generosity and kindness.

Riley turned and disappeared into his bedroom again, coming back with his piggy bank. After removing the plug from the bottom, he began shaking out all the loose change onto the family room couch. At this point, I had to sit down. It was too much! I wasn't sure my heart was capable of receiving so much love all at once. It actually made me feel uncomfortable. I couldn't let him sacrifice so much for me, could I?

I began to protest. "No, Riley, you save your money. Maybe there will be another time when you can help out with the cost of something."

But that sweet boy of mine wouldn't take no for an answer. He looked right into my eyes and ever so confidently asserted himself. "The time is now. I'm giving this money to you." Apparently, this was not up for discussion.

My daughter, Janie, who witnessed her brother's gift, ran to her bedroom. She, too, walked out with all her money in hand. Following the example set by her older brother, she opened her piggy bank, and before I could say anything, she began showering me with coins. As the coins rained down into my lap, I became overwhelmed with the sense that this was God pouring out His love for me. I simply had to sit there and take it all in. In that moment, I felt the perfect love of God taking the place of all my fear. I sensed that though I hadn't earned it and didn't deserve it, His love was for me—not to be refused, but humbly received. At that moment, I knew everything was going to be okay. My children would be taken care of, and I could stop worrying.

When the last coin from Janie's piggy bank finally fell into my lap, I thought of the story in Mark 12, of the poor old widow and what she gave to the church offering. As the story goes, "A poor widow came and put in two very small copper coins, worth only a few cents. Calling his disciples to him, Jesus said, 'Truly I tell you, this poor widow has put more into the treasury than all the others. They all gave out of their wealth; but she, out of her poverty, put in everything—all she had to live on'" (Mark 12:42–44). The poor widow had so little to give, but she was willing to risk it all without fear of the future—just as my children had just demonstrated to me. In the love of God, she knew she was safe and secure. As I reflected on her trust in God, I felt the Lord telling me in my spirit, *You must be willing to give it all.*

Minutes after giving me all her money, Janie handed me a little note. It read, "I love you so much I allowed myself to give up all my money for you. Love, Janie." As I read her sweet note, my heart melted. In my spirit, I heard God echoing, *I love you so much I allowed Myself to give up My life for you.* Tears began streaming down my cheeks.

Jesus willingly gave it all because of His love for each of us. He came that we might have life, and have it more abundantly (see John 10:10). Therefore, His abundant life—the love, freedom, blessings, joy, peace, and riches of His glory—is all for us! We don't have to earn it. He offers it to us freely! All He asks is that we open our hearts to receive it—to receive Him! Ultimately, the things God calls us to surrender now—our family's health and safety or our finances, for example—are small in comparison to the life God wants to bless us with. To receive all He has for us, we must first consider what we are holding on to, or trusting in other than God, and then be willing to let it go.

In Mark 10, we read a story with a different ending than the one above. This is the story of a man who disobeyed God's call to surrender:

> As Jesus started on his way, a man ran up to him and fell on his knees before him. "Good teacher," he asked, "what must I do to inherit eternal life?" "Why do you call me good?" Jesus answered. "No one is good—except God alone. You know the commandments: 'You shall not murder, you shall not commit adultery, you shall not steal, you shall not give false testimony, you shall not defraud, honor your father and mother.'" "Teacher," he declared, "all these I have kept since I was a boy." Jesus looked at him and loved him. "One thing you lack," he said. "Go, sell everything you have and give to the poor, and you will have treasure in heaven. Then come, follow me." At this the man's face fell. He went away sad, because he had great wealth.
>
> —*Mark* ***10:17–22***

Unfortunately, this man's wealth became a stumbling block in his relationship with the Lord. In choosing to hold on to his earthly possessions and pride rather than follow Jesus, he missed out on the greater blessing of the life he could have had with Jesus! How often do we struggle with the very same thing? We want to hold on to our possessions, control, pride, selfish ambition, and the pleasures of this world. We convince ourselves that these things are our salvation, that they will make us happy, keep us safe and secure, and grant us peace. However, they never do! That's because true fulfillment can only be found in following Jesus.

On the list of top ten things God warns us to steer clear of, idolatry is right there at the top. An idol is anything we allow to take the place of God. People often create idols for themselves as a coping mechanism for fear. It can be tempting to seek out security in something other than God when our circumstances feel so uncertain, to attempt to hold on to control in an uncontrollable world. The problem with this, other than the obvious sin of idolatry, is that we stop trusting God with our lives. We attempt to secure our own safety nets. We begin replacing God with things we think will bring us the happiness, comfort, safety, security, protection, and the healing we desire. We essentially tell God that we don't need Him and that we can manage everything ourselves.

Just about anything can become an idol—our significant other, children, money, career, authority figures, health, physical appearance, to-do lists, cleaning and organizing our homes, the praise and approval of man, food, etc. In reality, these things provide only temporary happiness. Before we know it, these idols we've turned to for some false sense of control begin controlling us. We become enslaved by them. The Bible says, "They themselves are slaves of depravity—for 'people are slaves to whatever has mastered them'" (2 Peter 2:19). If you are struggling with increased stress, anxiety, fear, relationship problems, and a taxed immune system, these are signs that you are not gaining control but losing it. Idols will rob us of time, health, money, ministry, and the opportunity to love and serve others. Anything we allow to control our lives or master us in some way is a potential idol that needs to be surrendered to God.

At some point in your walk with God, you will come to a metaphorical fork in the road, and you must decide once and for all whom you will serve. As Kyle Idleman put it in his book *Not a Fan*, "You won't be able to take the path of following Jesus without walking away from a different path." To live free from fear, you must learn to totally surrender at the foot of the cross all that you've been clinging to until now.

So often well-meaning people say, "Just let it go!" However, to a fearful heart, letting go of control can feel quite impossible! Letting go feels like a freefall off a cliff, a leap that is impossible to take. The thing is, you will not be able to let it all go until you learn to trust that God has you in the palm of His hand. Rather than struggling with yourself to simply *let go* of control in your own willpower—try picturing yourself placing all that you hold dear into God's strong, loving, caring, and capable hands. Pray and ask God to help you do this. God will help you break free from the grip of anxiety and fear attached to your fear of the future. Ask Him to confirm that this step is what He is calling you to do. Then, in faith and trust in God's sovereignty and good plan for your life, simply rest in the knowledge that He has your life under His control. Remember, you and all that you love are safe and secure in the palm of His hand. You can trust God with your heart.

Abraham, who was known as "the man of faith" (Galatians 3:9), experienced a fork-in-the-road decision when God told him to sacrifice his son, Isaac, on an altar to God. Now, you must understand: Isaac was the fulfillment of God's promise to make Abraham a father of many nations. Abraham already sacrificed his own earthly expectations before Isaac was born when he chose to believe in God's promise and power. Abraham could have questioned God, but he didn't. Instead, Abraham obeyed. He trusted that God knew what He was doing—and God proved Himself faithful. The day Abraham had planned to sacrifice Isaac, God provided a ram as a substitute, foreshadowing Jesus' substitution for us on the cross. You see, God never planned for Isaac to die; He only wanted to test Abraham's willingness to lay it all down in surrender. God wanted Abraham's heart. Will you, like Abraham, lay your Isaac down, whatever that may be?

Often the problem is we fear experiencing pain. Rather than trust God with our whole heart, we withhold it from Him. We put up walls of self-protection around it (another coping mechanism for fear). Unfortunately, those walls don't actually keep us from experiencing more pain. They do, however, keep us from experiencing the fullness of life Jesus died to give us. This only causes more anxiety and fear. To conquer anxiety and fear, we must learn to surrender our hearts fully to God and humbly receive His perfect love for us. It's only when we learn to rely on God's Word as truth, believing His perfect love as enough, that we will finally be able to surrender it all to Him.

Do you know the story of Shadrach, Meshach, and Abednego? These three God-fearing men were faced with a very difficult decision. King Nebuchadnezzar, under whom these men faithfully served, set up an image of gold—an idol. He insisted everyone bow down and worship it or be thrown into a blazing furnace. King Nebuchadnezzar said to Shadrach, Meshach, and Abednego, "If you are ready to fall down and worship the image I made, very good. But if you do not worship it, you will be thrown immediately into a blazing furnace. Then what god will be able to rescue you from my hand?" (Daniel 3:15).

To refuse the king's edict meant facing certain death. There was much to fear, but Shadrach, Meshach, and Abednego refused to bow down to fear. They would not bow to an image of gold, only to their God. They responded to the king's threats saying, "King Nebuchadnezzar, we do not need to defend ourselves before you in this matter. If we are thrown into the blazing furnace, the God we serve is able to deliver us from it, and he will deliver us from Your Majesty's hand. But even if he does not, we want you to know, Your Majesty, that we will not serve your gods or worship the image of gold you have set up" (Daniel 3:16–18).

I love that Shadrach, Meshach, and Abednego were so confident in God's saving power that they did not try to talk their way out of their situation. They did not fight the king's decision. They simply held fast to their convictions and refused to bow down to anything but God. They trusted in God's love for them—no matter the end result. God did not stop King Nebuchadnezzar from throwing Shadrach, Meshach, and Abednego into the fire because of their faith. Although they had to go through the fire, they did not go alone. Jesus met them in the flames and kept them from harm. Not one hair from their heads was singed.

After witnessing this miracle take place, King Nebuchadnezzar said, "Praise be to the God of Shadrach, Meshach and Abednego, who has sent his angel and rescued his servants! They trusted in him and defied the king's command and were willing to give up their lives rather than serve or worship any god except their own God . . . no other god can save in this way" (Daniel 3:28–29).

If you are going through the fire, know that Jesus is right there with you, and the flames will not consume you (see Isaiah 43:2). Do not turn to the right or to the left, but confidently walk the path that God has laid out before you. Remember, His grace is sufficient, and whatever God intends for you to walk through, He will be there to walk through it with you. This is His promise. It may not look like it, but this time of severe trial is actually the path leading you to the freedom and blessings I know you're praying for—that are found on the other side of your obedience to surrender.

In the midst of pain, it can be hard to see that God is still with us—that He still loves and cares for us—but God has not turned a blind eye to your pain. His heart is breaking for you.

"'I have heard your prayer and seen your tears,' says the Lord" (Isaiah 38:5). When it's hard to hold on to hope, remember David's confident assurance: you will "see the goodness of the Lord in the land of the living" (Psalm 27:13). No one can take from you what Jesus died to give to you: abundant life. Don't give up! God will restore you. He will repay you for the years the locusts have eaten. Nothing you have had to endure will be forgotten by Him or wasted within His kingdom. God is working all things together for your good, and His glory (see Romans 8:28). There is purpose in the pain, and there is a plan. "Weeping may endure for a night, but joy comes in the morning" (Psalm 30:5 NKJV).

Looking now to Jesus, our perfect example of total surrender, let's journey back to the moments just before His arrest in the Garden of Gethsemane, where He ultimately made the decision to surrender His life. It's there we will gain a clearer understanding of what God wants from us when He calls us to surrender:

> They went to a place called Gethsemane, and Jesus said to his disciples, "Sit here while I pray." He took Peter, James and John along with him, and he began to be deeply distressed and troubled. "My soul is overwhelmed with sorrow to the point of death," he said to them. "Stay here and keep watch." Going a little farther, he fell to the ground and prayed that if possible the hour might pass from him. "*Abba*, Father," he said, "everything is possible for you. Take this cup from me. Yet not what I will, but what you will." Then he returned to his disciples and found them sleeping. "Simon," he said to Peter, "are you asleep? Couldn't you keep watch for one hour? Watch and pray so that you will not fall into temptation. The spirit is willing, but the flesh is weak." Once more he went away and prayed the same

> thing. When he came back, he again found them sleeping, because their eyes were heavy. They did not know what to say to him. Returning the third time, he said to them, "Are you still sleeping and resting? Enough! The hour has come. Look, the Son of Man is delivered into the hands of sinners. Rise! Let us go! Here comes my betrayer!"
>
> —*Mark 14:32–42*

As I imagine the drama of this intense garden scene unfolding, I see Jesus demonstrating surrender in three ways. First, Jesus stayed in close communication with the Father so that He would not fall into temptation. Jesus warns us, "Watch and pray so that you will not fall into temptation. The spirit is willing, but the flesh is weak" (Mark 14:38). When we allow distance between ourselves and God, we are much more likely to give in to our own selfish desires because our flesh has the tendency to rise up in rebellion against the will of God. However, when we stay in close communication with the Father, by praying and reading His Word, He strengthens us by the power of His Holy Spirit to remain obedient to His will.

Second, Jesus persevered in prayer, according to the will of the Father. He prayed until the breakthrough came—until His heart and flesh were fully aligned with the Father's will. In the garden, we see that Jesus was overwhelmed and struggling emotionally with all that was about to take place. Although Jesus was fully God, He was also fully human. To overcome His flesh that was beginning to rise up, Jesus had to persevere in prayer. Luke 22:44 says, "And being in anguish, he prayed more earnestly, and his sweat was like drops of blood falling to the ground."

Isn't that just like what Paul tells us to do when we are anxious? "Do not be anxious about anything, but in every situation, by prayer and petition, with thanksgiving, present your requests to God" (Philippians 4:6). The struggle was intense, and yet Jesus never gave up praying. He didn't back down. In Mark 14, it says that Jesus prayed three times, "Not what I will, but what you will." I imagine His voice was tense as He continued to struggle with the heartache of knowing He would be rejected and abandoned by the ones He came to save, temporarily separated from the Father for the sins of the whole world, and forced to experience a gruesome, agonizing death. The first two times He prayed, He then found the disciples sleeping, and He spoke to them out of His distress. After Jesus finished praying for the third time, the tone of His voice changed. The breakthrough came! He was no longer in distress or struggling. Instead, we see Him strong, confident, and ready to do what He had been sent to do. To receive the strength and power we need to surrender to the Father's will, we too must persevere in prayer!

Jesus prayed and surrendered, but God's response was *not* to change His circumstances. At times, we pray for God to relieve anxiety or depression or any other kind of mental illness or painful circumstance, and we continue to struggle with it for years. We may have surrendered and believed God's truth, but we still find ourselves unable to break free, as if it's God's will. This was my experience. I struggled for years and years pleading with God and crying out to Him for relief from anxiety. At the same time, I was also crying out to Him for physical healing from a painful, chronic inflammatory condition. At times, I felt God didn't hear me. Knowing He could remove it in an instant, I couldn't understand why He would allow my suffering to continue for so long.

If this is your experience, I want to encourage you that our God *is* a God of deliverance. I will discuss this more in the next chapter. It's important to note here that I do not believe God will deny His children breakthrough from bondage to anxiety and fear. The Bible says, "For God has not given us a spirit of fear, but of power and of love and of a sound mind" (2 Timothy 1:7 NKJV). Could it be that your breakthrough is still on the way? Is it possible God is using your struggle with anxiety and fear to sanctify you and draw you closer to Him? What if the years of pain are preparing you to minister to others in their suffering? Like Jesus, you are called to persevere in prayer until the breakthrough comes—and it *will* come if you don't give up! Prayer changes things—not always our circumstances, but *always* our hearts.

Third, Jesus humbled Himself and became nothing. He was willing to lay down His life for all of us. Not because He had to, but because He *chose* to. Now, why would an all-powerful God do that? One word: love. In the moments just before Jesus' arrest, His perfect love for all of us was His motivation for total surrender. The Bible says, "For the joy set before him he endured the cross, scorning its shame, and sat down at the right hand of the throne of God" (Hebrews 12:2). To Jesus, the joy of bringing salvation to the ones He so deeply loved made surrendering to the humility and pain of death on a cross worthwhile. And what was the blessing found on the other side of His decision to surrender His life in the Garden of Gethsemane? He became the Savior of the World—and by His wounds, we are healed!

What might God be calling you to walk away from or surrender to Him at this moment? Jesus said, "Whoever wants to be my disciple must deny themselves and take up their cross daily and follow me. For whoever wants to save their life will lose it, but whoever loses their life for me will save it" (Luke 9:23–24). As Jesus' disciples, we are called to die to self daily and follow Him. It won't be easy, but you will never regret the decision to follow Him, wherever He may lead you. The indescribable peace, joy, and intimacy with God you get to experience when you choose Him above all else, and the promise of an eternity in heaven with Him, makes it all worth it! There's quite simply nothing and no one like our Jesus!

If you're wondering where your breakthrough is and looking for God's hand of blessing in your life, perhaps you'll find it on the other side of your obedience to surrender. Could it be there's more God is calling you to release that He has yet to reveal to you? If so, lift up your head and remember that Jesus took your place on the cross and paid the penalty for all your sin and pain. He took it upon Himself so you wouldn't have to bear the burden of it anymore! God will not let you fall. He has you in the palm of His hand. You can trust in the love He has for you. I picture Jesus saying now, *Child, give Me your sin. Give Me your anxiety and your fear. Give Me your pain. It's all right—come on now, give Me your pain.*

Will you choose to give up what is temporary for what is eternal? Are you ready to lay down your life—all your hopes, dreams, personal desires, and selfish ambition—for the One who gave His life for you? What about all your fears, insecurities, regrets, and past pain? Will you surrender those things as well? God can help you do this. When we choose to surrender our lives to Jesus, "In a twist of irony, we find that giving up our lives gives us the life we so desperately wanted all along" (Kyle Idleman, *Not a Fan*). We are all in a process of loosening our grip on the things of this world. One day we will depart from this world, and we will finally have to surrender it all. Until then, we should strive to keep an eternal perspective and an open hand. We truly have nothing to lose and everything to gain.

I have been crucified with Christ and I no longer live, but Christ lives in me. The life I now live in the body, I live by faith in the Son of God, who loved me and gave himself for me.

—*Galatians* ***2:20***

STEP 4:
SURRENDER YOUR LIFE AND LIVE FOR CHRIST

STUDY GUIDE

1. God wants to pour into you all the love He died to give you, but to receive His perfect love, your walls of self-protection must come down. Will you choose to trust God with your heart and surrender to His love for you? What practical step(s) can you take to demonstrate to the Lord your willingness to start moving in the direction of greater faith and trust in Him?

2. Jesus had to persevere in prayer before being led to the cross! Three times, Jesus prayed, "Not what I will, but what You will" (Mark 14:36). Jesus prayed until the breakthrough came. What does it mean to you to persevere in prayer? Is there something you know you need to persevere in prayer for?

3. Both breakthrough and blessing are found on the other side of your obedience to surrender. What is God calling you to surrender to Him?

4. Are you ready to die to self and live for Christ? No matter the cost? If not, what is holding you back from total surrender?

5. Read Mark 10:29–30 and James 1:12. How do these passages encourage you to keep an eternal perspective and an open hand with the temporary things of this world? What blessings are we promised when we give up our lives to follow Jesus?

PRAYER:

Heavenly Father, I confess that sometimes it's hard to follow where You lead. I don't always see the benefits when faced with suffering and trials of many kinds. I confess to You now that I have held back from surrendering my all to You. Please forgive me and help me to follow You with my whole heart. Help me to see that I can entrust everything to You without fear. Reveal to me those things I have yet to surrender, and give me the power to release them to You one by one. Thank You for willingly going to the cross for me. My salvation, joy, peace, purpose, and hope are in You alone. By Your wounds, I am healed! In the mighty name of Jesus, I pray, Amen!

STEP 5

BELIEVE—JESUS IS YOUR CHAIN BREAKER

Do not fear, only believe.

—*Mark 5:36 ESV*

Surrender and breakthrough go hand in hand. First, we surrender, then we experience a breakthrough. But what if you've gone through all the steps, surrendered everything you can think of, and yet true freedom feels just out of reach? I know the struggle feels overwhelming, and you've been fighting the good fight. You feel the chains of oppression refusing to shake loose and the hope you've been trying to hold on to slowly slipping away. At this point, you've probably started to wonder, *Where is God in all this?* While I don't know when or how your breakthrough will come, I do know God's promise is that He will bring you out of the darkness and break away your chains (Psalm 107:14). God has not abandoned you! In His perfect timing, Jesus, our chain breaker, will break through every chain of oppression holding you in bondage to anxiety and fear so that you may live in freedom and rejoice in Him—if only you believe!

The following story was one such chain-breaking experience I had with Jesus as He began to deliver me from anxiety and fear. While this deliverance occurred before beginning my five-year marked journey with the Lord, I can say with confidence that God used the pain of this circumstance to help me grow exponentially in my understanding of His perfect love.

It was Thanksgiving morning 2004, just three days after celebrating my first wedding anniversary with my husband, when I first felt the pain in my bladder. In the weeks and months that followed, the pain escalated rapidly. I endured six months of debilitating pain before any of my doctors were able to figure out what was going on and my pain was given a name: Interstitial Cystitis, a chronic inflammatory bladder condition.

I experienced a variety of symptoms, including but not limited to: excruciating pain in my bladder, a weakened immune system, allergies, chronic fatigue, food sensitivities, and extreme pain with sex. The pain never waned. I felt like my insides were on fire, and there was nothing I could do to squelch the flames. I fought intense feelings of guilt and shame for not being able to make love to my husband through all this. In addition, I began to see myself as defective, broken, and undeserving of his love. In this time of trial and testing, I really questioned where God was and why He hadn't stepped in to remove my pain.

My husband and I both struggled emotionally, silently wondering, *Will the pain ever get better? Will God choose to heal me? Will God heal our marriage?* It felt like an attack from the enemy on our marriage. The pain had driven a wedge between us. It was like a separation had occurred.

I struggled for months until one day, crippled by shame, pain, and the fear that my husband might one day leave me, I decided to get ahead of that fear and give my husband the opportunity to back out of our marriage—you know, should he decide this *new reality* wasn't for him. After a brief moment of reflection, he looked me in the eyes and said, "Sorry, you're stuck with me. I am never going to leave you. I love you!"

This was my moment of breakthrough. It was after hearing my husband's response that I realized, *I no longer need to fear losing him.* I had expected rejection and abandonment—and was even convinced I deserved it—but instead, my husband showed his commitment to our marriage and to unconditionally loving me. God hadn't walked away and left me in the midst of my pain. He was with me. He was with my husband too. I could finally let go of all that I had been trying to hold on to and control—my marriage, my health, my faith.

Up until this breakthrough moment in my life, deep down, I didn't believe I was loved! I mean, truly, unconditionally loved—even by God! I thought I had to earn love, and that if I missed the mark, love could be easily withheld or taken away. I had been striving to please others for most of my life because I so desperately wanted their love and approval. All the while, God was using this painful trial to teach me to rely on His perfect love and His power to rescue me. Through my husband, God helped me understand His kind of love is unconditional and unfailing! It's not a love dependent upon performance, but a love freely given, simply because of who God is. In my brokenness, God showed me that He would never reject me, abandon me, or stop loving me. This experience taught me that God moves and works in ways that will bring about the greatest good—even if that means allowing pain to continue for longer than we'd like.

One warning sign God may use to get your attention about hidden sins is physical pain. Read what the Anxiety and Depression Association of America said about the connection between anxiety and chronic pain:

> Muscle tension, body soreness, headaches. For people with anxiety disorders, pain like this may be all too familiar. Pain can be a common symptom—and sometimes a good indicator—of an anxiety disorder, particularly generalized anxiety disorder (GAD) . . . Many chronic pain disorders are common in people with anxiety disorders.

Harvard Medical School also published an article called "Pain, Anxiety, and Depression," stating:

> The overlap of anxiety, depression, and pain is particularly evident in chronic and sometimes disabling pain syndromes such as fibromyalgia, irritable bowel syndrome, low back pain, headaches, and nerve pain. For example, about two-thirds of patients with irritable bowel syndrome who are referred for follow-up care have symptoms of psychological distress, most often anxiety.

If you have begun to experience physical symptoms alongside anxiety with no clear physical cause, these could be warning signs that your mental state is wreaking havoc in your life. I encourage you to pay attention to these warning signs and consider how God may be using the state of your mental and physical health to communicate with you about your spiritual state. This is *not* to say that any physical pain you are experiencing is a result of anxiety or sin, but pain can be one of the ways God asks for your complete surrender.

While my breakthrough did not result in physical healing at that time, the spiritual healing I experienced was what God knew I needed most. This was not easy for me to accept. In thinking about my healing journey, both in the physical sense and the spiritual sense, there were times in the wait when I doubted a breakthrough would ever come. There were times I wondered, *Is deliverance and healing really possible, here and now? Why is it that some people seem to receive instantaneous breakthroughs, while for others, their breakthroughs continue to elude them? How can anyone pray for healing with confidence if healing isn't a sure thing?*

I wanted answers to these questions, not only for myself, but for all those in need of God's healing touch—whether physical, mental, or spiritual. To get God's perspective on these questions plaguing my mind, I went for a walk around my neighborhood. On my walk, I listened to the song "Chain

Breaker" by Zach Williams. The lyrics reverberated in my ears, reminding me that God is a pain taker, a way maker, and a chain-breaking Savior to all who call upon His name.

As I listened to the lyrics, I remembered the truth found in Psalm 103, and I discerned what God wanted me to understand about His promise of healing and deliverance:

> Praise the Lord, my soul, and forget not all his benefits—who forgives all your sins and heals all your diseases, who redeems your life from the pit and crowns you with love and compassion, who satisfies your desires with good things so that our youth is renewed like the eagle's. The Lord works righteousness and justice for all the oppressed.
>
> ***—Psalm 103:2–6***

The answer I felt the Lord was giving me was plain and simple—the Lord heals, and He delivers. Period. Did you know that the name *Yeshua*, which is the Hebrew form of Jesus, means "to deliver; to save; to rescue?" (Blair Parke, "Yeshua: Deliverer and Savior – Why This Name of God Is So Important for Today"). This is who our Jesus is! There is power in His name. By faith, we can believe that God will heal and deliver us. We can trust in His goodness, His plans, and His timing. We can release control without doubting for one second that we will receive everything we ask for in His name, according to His will. We can believe Jesus is our *chain breaker*. He is our healer.

But when will the breakthrough come? There may be times when you feel as though you will crumble under the oppressive weight of anxiety and fear. Oftentimes we see our enemy and immediately tremble, and say, *I'm not strong enough, Lord!* It may feel like you're reaching the end of your rope, but God is still on the throne. He has not forgotten you. He sees you,

He hears you, and He cares. So, friend, keep holding on and wait for the Lord. Keep crying out to God. Your deliverance is coming. You can count on it.

If you've ever felt like you weren't strong enough, you're not alone. It's in times of anxiety and fear that we must remember who God is: our very present help in time of need (Psalm 46:1). In the prophet Micah's time, the judgment of the Lord had come against Samaria and Jerusalem because of their ongoing sin and unrepentant hearts. It was a time of great calamity and destruction, of weeping and mourning. And yet, in the midst of such sorrow and suffering, God promised deliverance. He promised that one day a Savior would be born and save them from their sins—whom we know today as Jesus Christ! He spoke this through the prophet Micah to the people of Israel, saying: "The One who breaks open the way will go up before them; they will break through the gate and go out. Their King will pass through before them, the LORD at their head" (Micah 2:13).

This verse refers to Jesus as *the One who breaks open the way*—as in, He is Lord of the breakthrough! Although he didn't know when it would happen or how, this assurance from the Lord that the Israelites' breakthrough was coming gave the prophet Micah the confidence to declare by faith, "But as for me, I watch in hope for the LORD, I wait for God my Savior; my God will hear me" (Micah 7:7).

I want to believe like Micah, don't you? I want to be so confident in God's coming deliverance that I can stand firm in my faith and boldly declare it even when I cannot yet see the light. It's not always that easy, though, is it? To hold on to our faith and believe God will break through takes real conviction and fortitude. The chains of fear we're experiencing seem to mock our faith. They pressure us into keeping our eyes on our problems rather than on God. They try to push us to submit to our fears and give up on the hope we profess in Jesus, our Savior, to rescue us!

Fortunately, God gave us the story of Paul and Silas in prison to help us understand how to remain joyful in hope, patient in affliction, and faithful in prayer (see Romans 12:12) in the midst of our trials and suffering. In Acts 16:16–40, we read that these two disciples had just been severely beaten for testifying about Jesus, thrown into prison, and locked up in chains. I imagine the prison environment would have promoted hopelessness and despair: dark, dank, with the sounds of clanking chains and groaning from fellow inmates. How is it that Paul and Silas never gave up on God?

Unlike their fellow inmates, Paul and Silas were not without hope. They trusted God had a plan. Rather than give up, they began to sing! Rather than worry about their future or look to their chains in despair, Paul and Silas kept their eyes on God. They didn't sit in their jail cell panicking, complaining, or worrying. They didn't dwell on the pain they felt or consider the horrible way they had been treated. In their time of bondage, they chose to rise above their circumstances and believe that God was still with them and for them. As a result, in a place without hope, they became a source of hope and encouragement to others. In their worship to the Lord, they gave their fellow prisoners the courage to believe that they too had a Savior who loved them!

The story doesn't end there. Paul and Silas were still singing songs of praise to God, with the other prisoners listening in, when something miraculous happened: "Suddenly there was such a violent earthquake that the foundations of the prison were shaken. At once all the prison doors flew open, and everyone's chains came loose" (Acts 16:26). Wow! How great is our God! Paul and Silas trusted in the faithfulness of Jesus, their Savior, to break through their chains—and their faith, demonstrated through praise, opened the door for God to work a miracle in their midst. They got their breakthrough! As we can clearly see from this story, there is power in our praise to usher in the presence of the Lord. What is praise but an outward expression of our belief in Jesus Christ? By declaring our faith in Jesus to save us—through praise—I am confident we will see heaven invade earth and God move in power on our behalf.

Now, remember when I said God always works in ways that will bring about the greatest good? Not only did God deliver Paul and Silas and all the other prisoners from prison, but He allowed His breakthrough, miracle power to have a ripple effect. The story continues:

> The jailer woke up, and when he saw the prison doors open, he drew his sword and was about to kill himself because he thought the prisoners had escaped. But Paul shouted, "Don't harm yourself! We are all here!" The jailer called for lights, rushed in and fell trembling before Paul and Silas. He then brought them out and asked, "Sirs, what must I do to be saved?" They replied, "Believe in the Lord Jesus, and you will be saved—you and your household." Then they spoke the word of the Lord to him and to all the others in his house. At that hour of the night the jailer took them and washed their wounds; then immediately he and all his household were baptized.
>
> —*Acts* ***16:27–33***

Incredible! When the jailer saw all the prisoners' cell doors open wide and their chains broken off, he must have believed his worst fears were coming true! He was responsible for keeping prisoners. If they all had escaped, he would be held accountable, likely paying for his error with his own life.

With their chains broken off and their cell doors flung wide open, Paul and Silas could easily have made their escape without a moment's delay. Who would blame them for high-tailing it out of there? Rather than leave when they had the chance, I believe they recognized that true freedom is found in Jesus Christ alone. Even in chains, Paul and Silas were free. They must have discerned that the jailer was not. The jailer, though physically unbound, was nonetheless a captive to fear.

That night, Paul and Silas were called to extend the love of Jesus to the jailer so he could be set free from his fear of death, and he and his household were saved for eternity. All that was required for their deliverance was that they *believe in the Lord Jesus,* according to verse 31.

This was his breakthrough moment, the moment God had ordained for him from before the world began to come to the knowledge and truth of Jesus Christ. The veil was removed from his eyes, and for the first time, he understood the love of Jesus—the earth-shaking, chain-breaking power of His perfect love! Praise the Lord!

What if Paul and Silas had left prison the moment their chains came off and the doors opened? They would have missed the opportunity for God to use them to help save the jailer and his family. How devastating that could have been! Like Paul and Silas, we are also called to submit to God's perfect timing so the greatest good can be accomplished in and through us. What if the delay you're experiencing is for someone else's deliverance?

Jesus came to set the jailer free from his bondage to fear—and He will set you free too. Jesus has already gone before you and cleared the path paved for your deliverance from anxiety and fear. The Bible confirms this, saying, "Since the children have flesh and blood, he too shared in their humanity so that by his death he might break the power of him who holds the power of death—that is, the devil—and free those who all their lives were held in slavery by their fear of death" (Hebrews 2:14–15).

If Jesus gave His life so that *all* might be saved and live free from anything that would try to keep us in bondage, then you need only believe in Him to receive your deliverance! Why then as professed believers do many of us continue crawling through life riddled with anxiety and fear, unable to rise above it? Could it be we lack the faith that is needed to experience the miracle? The Bible tells us that when Jesus visited His hometown, "He did not do many miracles there because of their lack of faith" (Matthew 13:58). Have we, like them, failed to see Jesus for who He really is—the only one with the power to overcome death and raise to life?

As children of God, we ought to be straightening our crowns and walking out the victory we already possess in Jesus Christ, our Savior! Instead, I think we've been deceived by years of struggle and heartache, and we've exchanged the truth that God rescues for a lie. We've started believing the naysayers who shake their heads at us, and taunt, "Anxiety is just a part of who you are. Maybe this is your cross to bear. Anxiety is a chronic condition you will likely always struggle with." I'm sorry, but I don't believe that! Nowhere in the Bible does it say we should give up hope and stop believing in the power of Jesus Christ to break every chain that binds us!

The truth is anything that keeps us a slave to anxiety and fear is *not* of God! The Bible says, "God is love" (1 John 4:8; 1 John 4:16), and if we believe that "there is no fear in love, but perfect love casts out fear" (1 John 4:18 ESV), then we know we will be led continually in Christ toward complete freedom from fear.

I know it's so difficult to shake off unbelief, hopelessness, and fear—and to truly believe wholeheartedly when you feel like you are being dragged through the mud—but God's Word tells us to do just that! Isaiah 52:2 beseeches us: "Shake off your dust; rise up, sit enthroned, Jerusalem. Free yourself from the chains on your neck, Daughter Zion, now a captive." This verse is practically begging us to wake up and be free! Are you still pleading with God to give you the keys to unlock your cell door? I believe Jesus would say: *Look! You already hold the keys to the kingdom (see Mathew 16:19)! You don't have to live in fear anymore. Remember who you are: a child of God. You are My future bride! One day you will rule and reign with Me. Take up the authority you have been given in Me now and remove those chains weighing you down. Pick yourself up; dust yourself off. You were made for so much more!*

God has shown us through His Word how to live in the freedom He purchased for us with His own blood. If you're still living gripped by anxiety and fear, I believe James 4:7–10 could be the key that helps you unlock your chains and live free, here and now. It will teach you how to use the power and authority you've been given in Jesus Christ to walk out your freedom:

> Submit yourselves, then, to God. Resist the devil, and he will flee from you. Come near to God and he will come near to you. Wash your hands, you sinners, and purify your hearts, you double-minded. Grieve, mourn and wail. Change your laughter to mourning and your joy to gloom. Humble yourselves before the Lord, and he will lift you up.
>
> —*James 4:7–10*

While hard truth is difficult to receive, I want you to see that this Scripture offers hope for deliverance and incredible insight into how we can shake ourselves free from the grip of anxiety and fear. First, it says to *submit yourself to God.* In other words, obey Him! Do what is right. You must also *humble yourself*—giving up all worldly desires, self-interest, passions, and pursuits. Repent wholeheartedly, confessing your sins to God.

This may be an emotional process for you to finally recognize how your sin has hurt you, God, and others. It may result in grieving, mourning, and wailing over the weight of your sin—which would be a completely appropriate, even biblical response, also known as "godly sorrow" (see 2 Corinthians 7:10).

Draw near to God by seeking Him out in prayer, in the Word, and in fellowship with other believers. *Purify your heart* by aligning your thinking, attitude, and motives with His heart. Turn completely from wrong ways of thinking. No longer serve the devil's purposes, but *resist the devil* and commit to seeking and serving only the Lord. Turn from *double-mindedness,* which is saying you believe one thing while doing or thinking another, and the devil will finally leave! Allow the Holy Spirit to work on your heart through this sanctifying process to cleanse you from any unrighteous way of living, and you will experience the Lord's deliverance, peace, and joy!

The truth is, allowing ongoing, unrepented sin in our lives will keep us from the freedom and fullness of life Jesus died to give us (see John 10:10). It allows the devil a foothold into your life. Maybe you don't believe you have any ongoing sin issue. Or maybe you sense there is something you have not fully surrendered to the Lord, but you can't quite put your finger on it. If what I'm saying is resonating within your spirit right now, and you think maybe there is unconfessed sin in your life, start by examining your heart. Ask God for wisdom and discernment to see your sin. Our sin is often right in front of our face, a desire so deeply rooted that we have become blinded by it and put it ahead of our desire for God.

If the Holy Spirit is prompting you to seriously consider sin as a possible block to your deliverance, then start by asking yourself the following: *What is my true motivation behind my prayer requests? What am I seeking from the Lord? Is it something other than the Lord Himself? What am I still trying to control or protect that I have yet to trust God with? What am I still holding on to? Am I harboring beliefs in direct opposition with what the Word of God says? Do I doubt God's goodness?*

The Holy Spirit will bring clarity, revealing to you any unrepented sin in your life or blocks to healing and deliverance. A small adjustment in your thinking could be all you need to finally recognize where you've allowed yourself to be led astray. When your spiritual eyes are opened, you must choose to repent of whatever God has shown you before deliverance will come. If you need help with this, you can turn to the back of this book where I've provided "A Biblical Guide to Spiritual Deliverance." Remember, we are all sinners in need of a Savior. As humble followers of Jesus, we should all be quick to repent and confess our sins to the Lord!

If you are struggling with anxiety and fear, you will likely need to repent of choosing fear over faith—for believing the lies fear whispers over the truth of God's Word. I know it may be hard to admit to yourself that fear was a choice that you made. However, the Bible clearly tells us over and over again, *do not fear*. Look up the following verses, and you will begin to see what I mean: Isaiah 35:4, 41:10, 41:13–14, 43:1, 51:7, 54:4; Lamentations 3:57; Zephaniah 3:16; Haggai 2:5; and 1 Peter 3:6, 3:14. These verses remind us that we don't have to fear. God actually commands it in several of these verses, indicating that it is not only possible to *not* fear, but it is what He expects. Meaning, we can choose a different response other than fear. We can choose to believe instead! We can believe Jesus Christ has the power to save us and break the chains of every form of bondage and oppression we're experiencing. We can believe His perfect love is enough in any and every situation.

What if the root of fear is actually the sin of unbelief? Think about it. When we doubt God's goodness and refuse to take Him at His Word, we give the devil a foothold and allow fear to enter into our lives. When we react in fear because, at our core, we do not fully believe God will protect and provide for us, we allow fear to reign. As we continue to grasp for control in this uncontrollable world, we allow fear to take us captive. Then we discover the fear we thought we could control is, in fact, controlling us! Out of desperation, we work to manage the anxiety and fear that has us all tied up in knots, losing sight of the real problem—we don't fully believe God is who He says He is: the Redeemer and Savior of the world!

God in His mercy wants to lead us to repentance and heal us. To do this, God will use whatever means necessary to get our attention. Even if that means putting you in situations that cause your anxiety and fear to increase. He does not do this because He wants to see you suffer—quite the contrary! God loves you and wants to help you become aware of both your sin and your need for His deliverance. This is what is known as the *refiner's fire*—painful experiences that draw us closer to God and help conform us to His likeness. God simply loves you too much to let you continue to live your life a slave to fear.

When it comes to fear, the bottom line is this: without Jesus, there *is* reason to fear. However, when you have been washed in His blood, clothed in His righteousness, and covered by His perfect love, there is nothing left to fear! Jesus' broken body and spilled blood, which paid the price for your sins, is all that is needed for you to live victoriously each and every day!

Don't let your struggle with anxiety and fear continue to control you or keep you in bondage! Start praising Jesus for who He is—your chain breaker! Praise Him for the breakthrough He already has planned for you and the future He has prepared for you! Believe without doubting that He has the power to rescue you and that He intends to do it. Child of God, His grace is for you!

> Some sat in darkness, in utter darkness, prisoners suffering in iron chains, because they rebelled against God's commands and despised the plans of the Most High. So he subjected them to bitter labor; they stumbled, and there was no one to help. Then they cried to the LORD in their trouble, and he saved them from their distress. He brought them out of darkness, the utter darkness, and broke away their chains. Let them give thanks to the LORD for his unfailing love and his wonderful deeds for mankind, for he breaks down gates of bronze and cuts through bars of iron.
>
> ***—Psalm 107:10–16***

STEP 5:
BELIEVE—JESUS IS YOUR CHAIN BREAKER

STUDY GUIDE

1. We can learn so much from the way Paul and Silas chose to respond to their pain and suffering. What can you praise God for right now, even in the midst of your own pain and suffering?

2. Do you believe that to fear is a choice? Why or why not? Read again Isaiah 35:4, 41:10, 41:13–14, 43:1, 51:7, 54:4; Lamentations 3:57; Zephaniah 3:16; Haggai 2:5; and 1 Peter 3:6, 3:14.

3. Do you sense that fear and anxiety have become a stronghold in your life? Are you willing to seek spiritual deliverance through repentance, confession, and renouncing your sins? Consider using "A Biblical Guide to Spiritual Deliverance" in the back of this book for additional steps toward destroying strongholds in Jesus' name!

4. How does your belief in the gospel message of Jesus Christ and your knowledge of who Jesus is empower you to push back against fear and walk out your freedom in Christ? Read 2 Timothy 7–10 TPT.

5. Read Micah 2:13. This verse refers to Jesus as "the One who breaks open the way." He is the Lord of the breakthrough. Pray and ask Jesus to go before you and break open the way for your deliverance. Ask Him to lead you through the gate to your freedom!

PRAYER:

Heavenly Father, Thank You for Your amazing grace! Thank You for sending Your Son, Jesus, to pay the penalty for my sin and to make a way for my freedom from anxiety and fear. I confess that I have allowed fear to control my thoughts and actions, and I ask for Your forgiveness. I declare that You are Lord of my life, and I choose now to put my faith in You alone. Deliver me from oppression. Rescue me from my affliction. Save me from my sin. You are my strong deliverer. You are my help and my healer. You are my God. Your perfect love casts out all my fear. In You, I will overcome! Lord Jesus, go before me and break open the way. Break every chain. In the mighty name of Jesus and by the power of His blood, I pray, Amen!

PART II: THE RESTORATION

And the God of all grace, who called you to his eternal glory in Christ, after you have suffered a little while, will himself restore you and make you strong, firm and steadfast.

—1 Peter 5:10

STEP 6

EXPERIENCE PERFECT PEACE IN GOD'S PRESENCE

You will keep in perfect peace
those whose minds are steadfast,
because they trust in you.

—Isaiah 26:3

By grace, Jesus rescued you out of the darkness. Through His sacrificial work on the cross, you have been set free from bondage to anxiety and fear. Praise the Lord! Now, God wants to restore you, to make you strong, firm, and steadfast in your faith. You've already weathered many storms. At this point, you're probably looking for a place to let down your anchor and rest a while before continuing your journey. In this chapter, we will be taking some much-needed time to learn to sit at Jesus' feet—to renew our spirits, strengthen our faith, and experience perfect peace in His presence. We'll begin by taking time to offer thanksgiving and praise to the Lord for how far He has already brought us in our journey together toward living perfectly loved!

To celebrate and give thanks and praise to God for all that He had done for me, and as a public expression of my faith in Jesus Christ, I made the decision to be rebaptized. I sensed the Lord calling me to do it, so when the opportunity presented itself, I decided to go for it. I had been baptized as a child, but that was before I started truly walking with the Lord. This baptism would serve to memorialize the Lord's covenant faithfulness to rescue and deliver me. It would symbolize my death to sin and resurrection as a new creation in Christ. I was no longer captive to my sin of fear or to my old way of life. We had dealt with my sin together, and by the shed blood of Jesus, I had been set free. It was time to testify!

When the day finally came for me to be baptized, my family, friends, and church were all there to celebrate with me. Together, we rejoiced and marveled at the goodness of our great God! My baptism brought closure to my season of rescue, thereby signifying that a new season of life was upon me—a season of restoration.

For all those who persevere in following Jesus Christ, a time of restoration is coming! God promises us this in His Word, saying, "And the God of all grace, who called you to his eternal glory in Christ, after you have suffered a little while, will himself restore you and make you strong, firm and steadfast" (1 Peter 5:10). This is reason for us to celebrate!

How might you take some time before continuing your journey to commemorate and celebrate the amazing things God has done for you to bring you into this new season of restoration? Could it be writing out your testimony and sharing it with someone? Getting baptized or rebaptized? Or perhaps you'd like a visual memorial to God's faithfulness. Maybe a piece of faith art in your home, a stone in your garden, or a new tree planted in your yard? Maybe a gratitude jar you fill with notes of thanksgiving?

God is eagerly waiting to bless you with many good things, but don't forget to show your gratitude for all He has already done. Expressing our praise and thanksgiving to God is exactly how the Bible says we are to enter into His presence! "Enter his gates with thanksgiving and his courts with praise" (Psalm 100:4). There's good reason for this. As we discussed in the last chapter, praise often precedes breakthrough; however, there's so much more to praise than this.

Praise takes the focus off ourselves and our problems and puts it back on God, who is worthy of our time, attention, and praise. Praise keeps us humble. It reminds us that God is God, and we are not. Praise keeps us from complaining and being negative in our thoughts and talk. Praise opens the door to God's blessings. Praise increases our faith, refreshes our spirits, renews our minds, and transforms our hearts. It opens our eyes to God's goodness and prepares our hearts for worship.

Praise also increases our understanding of God's love for us. Praise invites God's presence.

When you feel disconnected from God, start praising Him for who He is, His unchanging character, and His promise to always be with us. Watch as the walls separating your heart from His come crashing down. When you feel defeated, disappointed, or frustrated by your circumstances, start praising God for all He has done for you and others, for His wonderful works for all mankind! His presence will strengthen your faith, refresh your spirit, and push back the enemy. When you feel rocked by the storms of life, and anxiety begins rising up within you, start praising God for the security you have because of His sovereignty. Declare by faith the good plans the Lord has for you! God has the power to reestablish you in His perfect peace.

Our heavenly Father welcomes us into His presence. Through the shed blood of Jesus Christ, we have been given 24/7 access into His throne room. This means nothing need keep you from experiencing Him or His perfect love for you. Mary, the sister of Martha and Lazarus, understood this. On three separate occasions, the Bible highlights for us Mary's commitment to putting Jesus first in her life. In all three interactions, we find Mary at the feet of Jesus—abiding in Him, crying out to Him, and adoring and exalting Him as Lord.

First, in Luke 10, we find Mary sitting at the feet of Jesus in the home of her sister, Martha. Jesus had been invited to dinner. While Martha became increasingly worried and upset because of the stress she was experiencing in preparing the meal, Mary was quite content to simply be with Jesus instead of serving her sister in the kitchen. This didn't go over well with Martha. She felt Mary was acting selfishly in not helping her with the meal prep and housework. She made sure to let Jesus know how she felt about it too!

Much to Martha's dismay, Jesus affirmed Mary's choice *to be* versus *to do*. "'Martha, Martha,' the Lord answered, 'you are worried and upset about many things, but few things are needed—or indeed only one. Mary has chosen what is better, and it will not be taken away from her'" (Luke 10:41–42). While Martha's intentions were good, her priorities were out of whack. She missed seeing what was most important—spending time with Jesus!

Okay, where are all my Marthas at? Have you ever struggled with Martha-like tendencies? I know I have. I'm much more of a Martha than a Mary. I struggle becoming distracted by my to-do lists. I stress when I think about all the things I need to get done. All the while losing sight of what is most important—taking time *to be* in God's presence. I'm still working on *being* versus *doing*.

Mary knew how to ignore distractions and be still before the Lord. She was able to discern that sitting at the feet of Jesus and experiencing peace in His presence was far more important than getting all the housework done. She didn't strive to meet others' expectations for her. She stayed committed to keeping Jesus first and foremost in her life.

The second time we hear about Mary being at the feet of Jesus, she is mourning the death of her brother, Lazarus. The Bible tells us, "When Mary reached the place where Jesus was and saw him, she fell at his feet and said, 'Lord, if you had been here, my brother would not have died.' When Jesus saw her weeping, and the Jews who had come along with her also weeping, he was deeply moved in spirit and troubled" (John 11:32–33).

Mary's gut response in her grief was to fall down at the feet of Jesus. I believe she knew that true comfort, peace, and joy are only found in Christ. Even life itself is only found in Jesus! We know she felt this way because she said to Jesus, "Lord, if you had been here, my brother would not have died" (John 11:32).

Filled with compassion for Mary, Jesus took time to comfort her in her grief—even knowing everything that was about to take place. Little did Mary know, but Jesus would soon raise Lazarus from the dead, and her tears of grief would become tears of joy!

Just as Jesus turned Mary's time of mourning into a time of celebration, He can turn your darkness to light, sadness to joy, pain to healing, insecurity to confidence, and all your fears and anxiety to perfect peace in His presence. In John 16:33, Jesus said, "I have told you these things, so that in me you may have peace. In this world you will have trouble. But take heart! I have overcome the world." Don't let the enemy steal your hope of a more joy-filled, beautiful, and abundant life. Brush off those grave clothes, sister! Clothe yourself in His resurrection power today and rise! Is anything too hard for Him?

The third time we see Mary, we find her unabashedly throwing herself at the feet of Jesus. This time she was in the home of her brother, Lazarus. He was hosting a dinner party for Jesus. While all the dinner guests were reclining at the table, John 12:3 says, "Mary took about a pint of pure nard, an expensive perfume; she poured it on Jesus' feet and wiped his feet with her hair."

Judas, the disciple who would later betray Jesus, raised a fuss. He argued that Mary had wasted the expensive perfume, which could have been sold for money to give to the poor. To Judas and maybe others, she looked a fool. But their approval was not her aim. To Mary, the act of pouring out the costly perfume on Jesus' feet was a tangible way for her to express her deep love, adoration, and reverence. She simply could not hold back from giving Him her all. Once again, Jesus defended Mary's actions, explaining to everyone present, "You will always have the poor among you, but you will not always have me" (John 12:8).

With eyes fixed on Jesus, and a heart full of love, Mary modeled for us how to worship Jesus—without worrying about what anyone might think. Jesus proved His commitment to all of us when He went to the cross to die for us. Now it's our turn to show our commitment—by pursuing Him and spending time in His presence.

Like Mary, may your love for Jesus produce a sweet aroma that draws others closer to Him. May you remember that your Jesus is more precious than all your worldly possessions—and His love and approval is far better than the love and approval of mankind.

In all three accounts, you'll notice that Jesus never once rebuked Mary for wanting to spend time with Him. He didn't say, *You know, Mary, you should really get up and start helping Martha. How else is everything going to get done in time?* He also didn't say, *Mary, why are you sitting here crying at My feet? Stop grieving and pull yourself together.* And Jesus never said, *Mary, why did you waste all that perfume? You've made a fool of yourself in front of everyone!* No, Jesus welcomed Mary into His presence with open arms, inviting her to come as she was and to simply receive love, comfort, help, protection, wise counsel, joy, and perfect peace. It was hers for the taking, anytime and anywhere.

In our relationship with God, I believe our enjoyment of His moment-by-moment presence in all we do matters more to Him than anything we could try to do for Him. Are we taking time to notice Him? God wants to spend time with us. He enjoys us! Are we showing gratitude for all that God has already done for us, or are we too busy trying to keep up with the things we still need to do? In our effort to please God, let's not lose sight of what is most important—staying present with Him.

Even if we have gone through the work of identifying triggers, confessing, and surrendering, without consistent time with the Lord, we will lose our focus on God. Rather than remembering to use our faith shields to deflect the wind and the rain, we'll make feeble attempts to withstand the storms of life in our own strength. This never works. Our fears end up growing bigger, louder, and stronger, and we become easily overwhelmed by the day-to-day struggles we face. In the following passage, let's look at how Jesus reacts to the storms of life as compared to His disciples:

> A furious squall came up, and the waves broke over the boat, so that it was nearly swamped. Jesus was in the stern, sleeping on a cushion. The disciples woke him and said to him, "Teacher, don't you care if we drown?" He got up, rebuked the wind and said to the waves, "Quiet! Be still!" Then the wind died down and it was completely calm. He said to his disciples, "Why are you so afraid? Do you still have no faith?" They were terrified and asked each other, "Who is this? Even the wind and the waves obey him!"
>
> —***Mark 4:37–41***

While Jesus remained perfectly at peace amid a raging storm, His disciples were quick to react in fear and panic. We can probably agree that our natural inclination is also to react in fear and panic, the way the disciples did. *Do you still have no faith?* Jesus asks us. Just like the disciples, Jesus doesn't ask us this question to shame us. Instead, I believe His question is meant to encourage us to put our trust and hope in God and ask ourselves, *What am I so afraid of?*

Are you believing and trusting in one moment and in the next doubting and afraid, still easily knocked down by waves of fear? Maybe you've experienced a breakthrough from the grip of anxiety and fear, but you find yourself still easily sucked back into it. Don't worry, Jesus will meet you right where you are in your faith journey to give you whatever amount of faith you need to succeed. You don't have to be strong all the time. You don't have to be perfect. Jesus promises to be with us in the storms of life. We can find comfort in knowing that we serve a God who is all powerful in our weakness, unafraid in our fear, and completely in control when life feels totally out of control.

Isaiah 26:3 says, "You will keep in perfect peace those whose minds are steadfast, because they trust in you." This is God's promise to us! When the storm is raging and chaotic winds thrash about, threatening your peace, Jesus is the anchor for your soul. He will be your shelter from the rain. He will keep you safe from the dangers of the rugged open sea, and whenever you start to drift, He will reel you back in. God will tether your heart to His when you fear you will drown, and rest assured, He will keep your little boat afloat. The Lord will command the wind and the waves to be still! He will lead you beside quiet waters (see Psalm 23:2). He will refill what the day's demands have emptied, refresh your spirit, strengthen your faith, and restore you to perfect peace in His presence.

In life, we can intentionally choose to take the path that will lead us closer to God, or we can let ourselves drift further from God's presence. If we allow ourselves to drift, we may someday find ourselves needing to be rescued all over again. If we remain close by His side, however—as sheep under the protection and care of a shepherd—we will experience God's perfect love and peace, and we will thrive.

In Psalm 23, King David poetically paints a beautiful picture for us of how Jesus, the Good Shepherd, watches over us and lovingly cares for us as the sheep of His pasture. Let's take some time to soak in all this psalm has to teach us:

> The LORD is my shepherd, I lack nothing. He makes me lie down in green pastures, he leads me beside quiet waters, he refreshes my soul. He guides me along the right paths for his name's sake. Even though I walk through the darkest valley, I will fear no evil, for you are with me; your rod and your staff, they comfort me. You prepare a table before me in the presence of my enemies. You anoint my head with oil; my cup overflows. Surely goodness and love will follow me all the days of my life, and I shall dwell in the house of the LORD forever.

Our Good Shepherd is providing, restoring, leading, comforting, protecting, and sacrificing for us so that we may live as abundantly blessed and loved sheep all the days of our lives. In Christ, we lack nothing. Our hopes, dreams, and longings for something more will all be met in the power of His presence. He calls to us from the deep, gently whispering our name, offering us rest in a world full of chaos. He is our protection, and we will find comfort and security in knowing He is looking after us every moment of every day. With indescribable peace, our Good Shepherd blesses all those who walk with Him and follow His ways.

Jesus came that we might "have life, and have it to the full" (John 10:10). He invites us to join Him at His Father's banquet table to feast on the bread of life—His body that was broken for us—and be filled. He invites us to drink deeply from the cup of His blood, which continually overflows with amazing grace and perfect love for us. Our heavenly Father has withheld nothing from us! Will you accept the King of King's invitation to join Him at His banquet table? He has called you, chosen and reserved a place of honor for you. He has prepared His finest. As a child of the King, heir to His eternal kingdom, you are privy to the blessings thereof. "Taste and see that the LORD is good; blessed is the one who takes refuge in him" (Psalm 34:8).

At times this banquet table of blessing may not feel so blessed. Especially when you come to the table having experienced hardship, pain, or loss in this life. Oh, how quick we are to pull away from God and push back from His table when we are hurting. However, don't we need His blessing most during hard times? We forget that giving thanks and praise and spending time in God's presence aren't just for when our circumstances are palatable and His goodness is tangible to us. Thanksgiving should fill our hearts every day and in every season (see 1 Thessalonians 5:18), not just on holidays and special occasions or when we feel like it. We can give thanks to the Lord perpetually because His goodness can be found in everything—even in brokenness, grief, and unfulfilled hopes and dreams.

God is good all the time. When we open our eyes to His grace and pursue His loving presence, we *will* see His goodness and experience His peace. Let your thanksgiving flow, and the joy of the Lord will begin to bubble up within you, reminding you of God's loving presence and His power to restore you to perfect peace.

Without doubt, the abundant life can only be experienced in God's presence. However, *how* we experience God is not one-size-fits-all! As followers of Jesus Christ, we have been created to connect with God in a variety of ways. While we all have the capacity to connect with God when we read His Word, pray, and praise Him, how that looks for each of us, as individuals, can vary significantly. Knowing how God has uniquely created you to be drawn into His presence, and to learn and grow in your faith, will help deepen your relationship with Him.

We may experience God's manifest presence in any number of ways, but the following descriptions and examples may help you to identify some of the ways you most readily and intimately connect with Him. Also, keep in mind that how you best connect with God can change over time and in different seasons of life. You don't have to get stuck in any one approach. This is certainly not a comprehensive list, but one I put together based on my personal experience, research, and what others have shared with me. Think of it, instead, as a starting point to understanding your connection with the Lord:

- *The Extrovert* loves fellowshipping with other believers. Social interactions spark joy and excitement, giving this individual the opportunity to build on others' enthusiasm and faith. She feels closer to God when with other people.
- *The Server* loves serving and caring for others. In making meals for a family in need or helping out at a church function, this individual is energized, and filled with the presence of God.
- *The Artist* loves using their ingenuity and creativity to create or build something. Writing a song, choreographing a dance routine, creating a sculpture or painting, producing a film, and designing a house are all examples of how this individual enjoys connecting with God.
- *The Worshipper* loves listening to music, singing, and/or playing instruments. This individual is drawn quickly into God's presence through music.

- *The Intellectual* loves any opportunity to learn. This individual prefers to dive into books and study rich text about the Bible, history, government, languages, science, and so on to connect with God.
- *The Contemplative* loves spending time deep in thought, contemplating the mysteries of life. In taking extended amounts of time for personal reflection, reading or listening to God's Word and other books that encourage their spiritual growth, and prayer, this individual feels closest to God.
- *The Naturalist* loves being in nature and connecting with God outdoors. In admiring the beauty of God's creation—seeing the sights and listening to the sounds—this individual feels closest to God.

If you don't think you connect with God in any of these ways, keep seeking! A great article about finding your unique worship style is "The Ultimate Guide to Connect with God," written by Asheritah Ciuciu. In it, Asheritah gives hundreds of ideas for the 12 different modes of connecting with God she's identified.

One of the ways I connect most readily with God is through praise and worship music. It's like kindling to the Holy Spirit's fire within me. It moves me to worship, then to read my Bible, pray, and journal my thoughts. It helps me hear God's voice more clearly. In fact, one of the ways God first called me to Himself was in a song. For me, the right song can be as transformational as a powerful sermon! I love adding new songs to my music library and creating playlists for the various seasons of life I'm in. (Check out my Living Perfectly Loved Playlist on my website.) Music has been a gift from God to me, even though I am not particularly gifted at singing or composing it myself. Through music, the Lord has drawn me closer to Himself—one song at a time!

My daily quiet time routine often begins with worship. I turn on my worship playlist, and I sing songs to God, lifting up each word to God in prayer. While I'm singing, God often begins speaking to my heart. He puts certain words or thoughts in my head. This is when I turn to my Bible and start reading. Sometimes I read systematically through a book of the Bible. Other times, I'll use a study guide or Bible reading plan in my Bible app to guide me through. I'll look up Bible commentary online or begin a word search in my Bible app for the words or phrases I feel God speaking to me, and then read through the scriptures that pop up. Whether using my printed Bible or a digital version to dive into God's Word, I'll underline, write notes, and highlight what stands out to me in the text. Then, I'll spend a little time journaling what God has put on my heart. I'll record my own thoughts and various Bible verses I want to remember. Finally, I pray as I feel led, for myself, my family and friends, my church, my kids' school, government leaders, etc. I'll confess my sins and thank God for the time I got to spend with Him, and for strengthening and leading me to fulfill His plans and purposes for my life.

Where can you go to meet with God? God is ready and willing to meet with us anywhere. You may find it helps you, though, to designate a specific place in your home to meet with Him. Ideally, away from chaos and distractions. Should the ideal space not be readily available, you can still meet with God wherever you are. If you are a mother of young children or live in tight quarters with a big family, I realize finding any quiet space may prove to be quite challenging. In this case, bring the people in your life close to you to share in the experience of reading God's Word and praying. There is nowhere the

Holy Spirit can't reach you. Nothing can separate you from God's presence or His love (see Romans 8:38–39).

One of my favorite places to get away and spend time with the Lord is outdoors in nature. When I stop to look up at the sky, I take notice of openings in the clouds that appear like portals to an open heaven. I praise Him for all He has created and for the opportunity to sense His nearness. When I hear a singing bird or see a beautiful butterfly float by, I know that God is with me. The rainbow after the rain reminds me of God's promises and His faithfulness. Amid gentle breezes rustling through the trees on a hike or relaxing by the ocean waves crashing and bubbling up the shoreline, I see heavenly displays of His beauty and greatness. I feel Him in the warmth of the sunshine on my skin, with its brilliant rays shining down on my face. I close my eyes and soak it all in. God is in it all, if only we take the time to notice Him.

When do you connect with God? God is always present and available to meet with us. Often when we feel distant from God, it's our social calendars, overstuffed schedules, upside-down priorities, and lack of discipline that are getting in the way of regularly entering into His presence. If meeting with God on a consistent basis has been a struggle for you in the past, you may find it helpful to set aside a specific time each day to meet with Him, in the same way you might create space in your schedule to meet a friend for lunch or coffee.

Some women I know prefer to meet with God first thing in the morning. Taking this approach ensures their day gets off to a good start, and it helps them to avoid any distractions that might later interrupt their time with the Lord. Still others prefer to spend time with God in the evening; this is when they feel most relaxed and able to focus, or this is when they have the most available time. What's important is not the hour of the day, but the quality of the time you spend together. We want to give God our best, not our leftovers. When our hearts aren't really in it, we end up going through the motions just to be able to say that we did it. That's not what God wants, and it likely won't lead to experiencing more of God's peace either.

I typically choose to have my quiet time with God in the morning, just as soon as I'm awake enough to focus. However, I also tend to find pockets of time throughout the rest of my day to pray, read articles or books that encourage my spiritual growth, and journal the things God has been saying to me or teaching me. I include my kids as well. Most every weekday, we do a short 10–15 minute devotional as a family. We've used RightNow Media videos, various Bible reading plans, and devotional books over the years. We briefly discuss the material we cover, and then we end our time by praying together. My routine and the amount of time I spend continues to change with each new season of life. I've discovered that the quantity of time and materials isn't very important—rather it's that I commit to spending dedicated time with the Lord every day: unrushed, concentrated, heart open, and vulnerable to Him.

God can be found and experienced in countless ways! Keep your spiritual eyes open and watch for God to show up in your day-to-day routines and mundane tasks. He's in the everyday chores, like the piles of laundry and dishes needing to be cleaned. You can find Him in the kindness of a stranger. He's in casual conversations that turn into opportunities to share the love of Jesus. He's in the love and faithfulness of your family and friends.

We can meet with God anytime and anywhere. The when, where, and how of your experiencing God may be vastly different from mine, but the most important thing is that you experience Him. First, by entering into His presence with thanksgiving and praise. Then, by taking time to sit at His feet—in His Word and in prayer—to get filled back up, renew your spirit, strengthen your faith, and be restored to perfect peace.

Although we cannot physically sit at the feet of Jesus or share a bench with Him in a fishing boat, we have the gift of the Holy Spirit, the fount of every blessing, with us always to lead us on our journey. As you enter into your season of restoration, I pray you see before you an open door to heaven and hear the Lord saying to you, *Come up here!* Then, as you move to higher ground, may God give you a deeper understanding of who He is, what He has done for you, who you are in Him, and how profoundly and passionately He loves you!

> The Spirit and the bride say, "Come!" And let the one who hears say, "Come!" Let the one who is thirsty come; and let the one who wishes take the free gift of the water of life.
>
> —*Revelation 22:17*

STEP 6: EXPERIENCE PERFECT PEACE IN GOD'S PRESENCE

STUDY GUIDE

1. Why is it important to give thanks and praise to God? Describe at least three ways thanksgiving and praise prepare our hearts to enter into God's presence.

2. Read Luke 10:38–42, John 11:32–33, and John 12:1–8. Which interaction between Jesus and Mary stands out to you the most, and why? How might you apply what Mary modeled in her relationship with Jesus to your own relationship with Him?

3. How do you experience God?

4. Where can you go to meet with God?

5. When do you prefer to meet with God?

6. Create your own praise and worship playlist of at least 10 songs. (If you need song recommendations, you can check out my Living Perfectly Loved Playlist on my website.)

PRAYER:

Heavenly Father, Thank You for being with me in the storms of life, commanding the wind and the waves to be still, and leading me beside quiet waters with You. Restore my soul. Lead me along the right paths for Your name's sake. When fear threatens my peace, help me feel Your presence and trust in Your unfailing love. There is perfect peace in You and fullness of joy in Your presence. Help me to put You first in my life and make meeting with You daily more of a priority. I want to be closer to You. I praise Your name and worship You alone! In Jesus' name I pray, Amen.

STEP 7

REBUILD YOUR IDENTITY AND SECURE YOUR FAITH IN CHRIST

See, I lay a stone in Zion, a tested stone, a precious cornerstone for a sure foundation; the one who relies on it will never be stricken with panic.

—*Isaiah 26:18*

God will reestablish us in His perfect peace each and every time we enter into His presence. We can retreat to Him and find shelter from the storms of life any time we choose. However, if every time we leave the safety of our prayer closets we find ourselves stricken with panic, we must then ask ourselves, *Have I truly learned to rely on Jesus Christ, the Rock of my salvation, as my one sure foundation?*

Perhaps we have placed our hope in something that can be burned up, used up, broken, or removed. Perhaps our faith is dependent upon our own strength or ability or that of someone else. If our foundation rests on something temporal, or of this world, we will likely find ourselves right back where we started—slaves to anxiety and fear. To remain free from anxiety and fear, we need a mature faith. One that will stand through trials and storms. Rock-solid faith built on a sure, eternal foundation. With our feet firmly planted upon Jesus Christ, and with His Word rooted deep within our hearts, we will not be shaken.

Before learning the truth of God's perfect love for me, before finding my identity in Christ, I would get up to look in the mirror each morning and count the many blemishes and imperfections I saw staring back at me. It was frustrating and embarrassing to still be struggling with acne into my thirties. No matter how many different products and treatments I'd tried over the years, I continued to battle bad breakouts. I pleaded with God to take it away. I was tired of fighting it, of trying to control my problem skin. But God continued to allow acne to afflict me, despite my desperate pleas.

In the midst of my frustration, helplessness, and shame, I couldn't see that who I was in Christ mattered more than whether or not I had clear skin. I only saw someone who didn't measure up on the outside. I'm guessing this is why God did not take my skin problems away—He couldn't have me believing my self-worth was only skin deep. Unfortunately, I couldn't let it go. As a result, I battled insecurity for years.

Starting in my teen years, I turned to makeup in an effort to conceal the imperfections on my face. I thought if I could cover up my flaws, people would be more likely to accept and love me. With makeup on, I felt confident and beautiful. Without it, I felt unworthy and ashamed. It wasn't long after starting to wear makeup that I no longer felt comfortable in public without it. I began avoiding social situations where I couldn't cover up with makeup, such as the beach or pool. I stopped looking people in the eye for fear I would catch them staring at my broken-out skin and feel humiliated. I didn't realize I was establishing a dependency on makeup—a dependency that would lead to a fear of letting others see the real me.

All this striving for perfection and control opened a door for pride to grip my heart. I didn't recognize my pridefulness at first because it masked itself as anxiety and fear. But where fear was present in my life—telling me that others would reject the real me—pride was not far away. I was surprised to discover some of the anxiety I was experiencing was actually a pride issue at its core because I had never equated insecurity with pride. But what I discovered is insecurity is self-focused rather than others-focused. God began revealing to me that in order to gain complete victory over anxiety and fear, the sin of pride had to also be removed.

It was wrong for me to build my identity and self-worth upon foundation makeup rather than the foundation of my faith, Jesus Christ. It wasn't until years later, on this journey with the Lord to overcome anxiety and fear, that I sensed God calling me to stop wearing makeup. He gently revealed that it was time to remove the mask. I had heard God telling me this in the past, but I was never willing to listen to Him. This time around, I suppose I was a little more open. Or maybe a little more desperate for healing.

I heard God saying, *Stop letting the mirror tell you who you are. Stop believing its lies. Let Me tell you who you are in Me. Don't look to the world, which says you don't measure up, which says you aren't enough. In Me, you are enough. "For by one sacrifice [I have] made perfect forever those who are being made holy" (Hebrews 10:14).*

It was time for me to find out who I really was, to let others see the *real* me, and to learn to love myself. At first, I tried to ignore God's still, small voice again. Honestly, I wasn't sure I could commit to giving up wearing makeup completely. It would feel like walking out my front door stark naked, completely exposed. However, His voice persisted. It was July 4th, Independence Day, when I heard Him say, *Cover up your bathroom mirror and tape Scripture to it. Declare your independence from makeup today!*

I thought, *My husband is going to think I'm absolutely crazy! God, there is no way I can actually do this.* Still, I couldn't shake the conviction I felt in my spirit. So after mustering up as much courage as I could, I told my husband what I had been thinking about doing. His response took me completely by surprise: "You've struggled with this for a long time. I think it might be a good idea. You're beautiful with or without makeup."

What a sweetheart! His response was confirmation to me that I wasn't, in fact, hearing things and losing my mind. God was in this! Why else would my husband agree to let me cover up all the mirrors in the house with plastic tablecloths and post Scripture to keep me from looking in the mirror, criticizing myself, and picking at my skin? I mean, come on. Seriously?

As much as I didn't want to go through with it, I knew I needed to be obedient to follow God's leading. Plus, I really wanted to be free from my bondage to makeup. Thus, not a drop of primer, foundation, concealer, mascara, eyeliner, eyeshadow, blush, or even lip gloss touched my face for a whole year and a half. I didn't cheat once—not even with a tinted moisturizer, translucent powder, or clear lip gloss, tempting as it was.

It was difficult to do at first. I felt very insecure, and I feared what people might think or say to me. God met me in my insecurity, though, and reassured me I was doing the right thing with the truth of His Word. He showed me Isaiah 54:4, which says, "Do not be afraid; you will not be put to shame. Do not fear disgrace; you will not be humiliated."

Much to my surprise, I never once heard a negative remark about my appearance the whole year and a half I fasted from makeup. Instead of being shamed and rejected, I experienced tremendous freedom and healing! I learned that people didn't just love the me who seemingly had it altogether, but the *real* me—imperfections and all! A huge weight was lifted, one I didn't know I had been carrying around with me for far too long.

Unmasked, I learned to receive the love, acceptance, and approval that was mine in Jesus Christ. As a result, I grew more confident in who I was in Him. During the time of my makeup fast, I learned to stop letting the mirror tell me who I was, and God rebuilt my identity and self-worth upon the sure foundation of Jesus Christ, according to His Word—*not* foundation makeup. God revealed to me that I was loved, beautiful, flawless, and clothed with the perfection of Christ.

He took away my fear of rejection with the promise of His unfailing love, and He showed me His plans for my complete restoration.

Mark Batterson writes in his book *Soulprint*, "Scripture is the only perfect mirror because it reveals how our Designer sees us. Most of our identity problems are the result of looking in the wrong mirrors."

It's not uncommon for those who struggle with anxiety and fear to attempt to mask their weaknesses. Unbeknownst to them, this is how the enemy shames them into establishing a performance-based identity. A performance-based identity centers a person's life and self-worth around what they can accomplish and control in their own strength. Someone whose identity and self-worth are built upon their performance believes their works are what make them who they are. Driven by pride and fear, they start believing they need to do more, achieve more, and be more to prove themselves worthy of man's praise and God's love. Ultimately, fallible human effort and works are an unstable foundation. Attempting to control and strive your way into worthiness essentially denies that the work of the cross of Jesus Christ is enough.

Pride is similar to fear in that pride tells us to be concerned about what others think of us and to not let anyone else in. Pride says we should only let others see the best version of ourselves, the version that seemingly has it all together, the highlight reel we don't mind sharing on social media. Pride boasts: *I am in control of my own life. I will determine how to live my best life. I don't need anyone else's help. I've got this!* The problem is we don't "*got this.*" Control is nothing more than an illusion. Truth be told, we're afraid to surrender our perception of control to God. We worry about what He might require of us or ask us to give up if we did.

Pride is often the last besetting sin to go when it comes to anxiety and fear because pride takes away our ability to discern and hear God clearly, making it hard even to recognize that pride is at work within us. To uproot pride, we must learn to relinquish control of our lives to God. Yes, this means surrendering our lives to Him, again. We must humble ourselves before God and say, *My life is not my own. I was bought at a price. I choose to live my life for You, God.*

Our worth is not self-made; it cannot be found in any of the following: our job titles, our relationships with others, our parenting skills, our net worth, our physical appearance, our list of accomplishments, the good works we do, the number of volunteer hours we work, the success of our ministry, or even how well-versed we are in Scripture. Our worth is found in being adopted daughters of our heavenly Father (see John 1:12; Romans 8:15; Ephesians 1:5; and 1 John 3:1). It is found in who we become in relationship with Christ. The death of Jesus on the cross allows us to proclaim, *I am loved because Jesus Christ found me worth dying for!* The end.

Right before Jesus breathed His last breath here on earth, He declared, "It is finished!" (John 19:30). Therefore, since His death and resurrection are final, and there is nothing anyone can do to improve upon or add to what He already accomplished, we ought to start believing that who we are in Christ is truly enough! According to the Word of God, we are children of God (see Galatians 3:26), heirs to a kingdom not of this world (see Romans 8:17; John 18:36), chain breakers (see Isaiah 58:6), the salt of the earth (see Matthew 5:13), the light of the world (see Matthew 5:14), chosen, holy, and dearly loved (see Colossians 3:12), wonderfully made (see Psalm 139:14), altogether beautiful and flawless (see Song of Songs 4:7), and the bride of Christ (see Revelation 21:9). All this, God says, and more!

If our faith is built upon a foundation of false beliefs—misconceived notions about who God is, what He has done for us, or who we are in relationship with Him—then we are likely living as unbelievers on some level, deprived of the fullness of life we could be living in Christ. For this reason, it is vital we rebuild our identities and secure our faith on the sure foundation of Jesus Christ.

My experience has taught me that the primary way this is accomplished is through the reading and hearing of God's Word. Not only will you find peace in His presence, as we learned in Step 6, but His truth will penetrate your heart. As you allow God's Word to grow deep roots and dwell within you, you will gain greater understanding of who God is, what He has done for you, and who you are in Him. This understanding will consequently establish your identity and secure your foundation of faith in Christ.

Paul put it this way: "Then, by constantly using your faith, the life of Christ will be released deep inside you, and the resting place of his love will become the very source and root of your life" (Ephesians 3:17, TPT). Then you can begin using your faith to step out and take action as God leads you, confident that His perfect love can be counted on in all things. And you will discover as God establishes and perfects His love within you that fear cannot exist; it is driven out (see 1 John 4:18). Hallelujah!

To begin the process of becoming deeply rooted in God's perfect love, we must first examine whether our hearts are open to receiving His Word. Jesus helped His disciples do this by sharing the parable of the sower with them. In this parable, Jesus explained to them the importance of examining the condition of their hearts to ensure the seeds of God's Word take root and grow spiritual fruit. Jesus said:

> A farmer went out to sow his seed. As he was scattering the seed, some fell along the path, and the birds came and ate it up. Some fell on rocky places, where it did not have much soil. It sprang up quickly, because the soil was shallow. But when the sun came up, the plants were scorched, and they withered because they had no root. Other seed fell among thorns, which grew up and choked the plants. Still other seed fell on good soil, where it produced a crop—a hundred, sixty or thirty times what was sown.
>
> —*Matthew* ***13:3–8***

According to the parable, there are four types of soil, each one representing the different ways people respond when hearing the gospel of Jesus Christ. First is the hard ground, or the heart that is hardened to the Word of God. This individual is not able to receive God's Word at all. The seeds of God's Word are quickly snatched away by the enemy. Second, the rocky ground. In rocky soil, the seed is received. The plant quickly sprouts up but soon withers because there is no depth to the soil. This is like those who hear the Word and like what they hear, but because the Word of God is not deeply rooted in their hearts, when difficult circumstances arise in their lives and their faith in God is challenged in some way, they are quick to turn from their faith. Their faith shrivels up, much like a sun-scorched plant. Third is the seed that fell among thorns. This represents the person who receives the Word but becomes distracted by the pleasures of this world. Eventually temptation takes over and chokes out the Word. And last, the good soil is like those who receive the Word and take it to heart, allowing it to grow deep roots, thereby securing their faith in Christ. The seeds of the Word planted in good soil grow and increase, producing fruit in their lives and in the lives of those they touch.

As we reflect on the parable of the sower, we ought to be asking ourselves whether the seeds of truth and wisdom God plants in us through His Word will cultivate spiritual growth and bear spiritual fruit? The fruit produced from the good soil is the fruit of the Spirit (love, joy, peace, patience, kindness, goodness, faithfulness, gentleness, and self-control—see Galatians 5:22–23). When we bear spiritual fruit, it is evidence of true salvation in Jesus Christ and of the transforming work of the Holy Spirit (see Matthew 7:20). If we lack evidence of the fruit of the Spirit in our lives, or if we've stopped producing spiritual fruit, we should stop and pray, asking God to help His Word take root and grow down deep into our hearts that our fruit may multiply!

Did you know that forests depend upon wildfires for regeneration and renewal? Wildfires burn away overgrowth and enrich the soil on the forest floor, allowing for new growth to occur, providing opportunity for a forest to thrive all over again. Likewise, God knows that times of pain and struggle are sometimes necessary to prepare our hearts to receive the seed of God's Word, from which new spiritual growth can occur. Oftentimes, it's in our most difficult seasons of life that we will see the greatest amount of spiritual growth take place.

If you're in a season of life where God is allowing Satan to "sift you like wheat" (Luke 22:31), you can trust that nothing happening to you is done without God's express permission (see Lamentations 3:37). And "though he [God] brings grief, he will show compassion, so great is his unfailing love. For he does not willingly bring affliction or grief to anyone" (Lamentations 3:32–33). God wants you to become the *good soil* He always intended you to be so that you will bear much spiritual fruit. He will use this season of potentially painful regeneration and renewal to help you get rid of any rocky soil or thorns that may be hindering your spiritual growth and to soften the soil of your heart to receive more of Him. Let His work in you be done. Hold fast to His Word! A time of budding and blossoming is surely on its way.

In times of renewed anxiety or fear, do not give in to shame or doubt that your breakthroughs were real. Instead, be open to receiving more of God's grace. Do you know that His grace is holding you even now? The Bible says, "The eternal God is your refuge, and his everlasting arms are under you" (Deuteronomy 33:27 NLT). You are safe and secure in His grip. In your weakness, His grace is strong. In your insecurity, His grace gives you confidence. In your lack, His grace supplies all you need. In your anxiety and fear, His grace reassures you of His steadfast, perfect love that will see you through to complete victory!

While God is full of grace and love for us, the sole intention of our adversary, the devil, is to stand before God accusing us night and day of all kinds of wrongdoing. He will heap such condemnation and shame upon us that, at times, we may start to doubt our identity in Christ—that we were chosen by God before the creation of the world to be saved for eternity (see Ephesians 1:4–5). If the fear of losing your salvation has ever gripped your heart, let me reassure you that your salvation in Christ is secure. When you became a Christian, Jesus Christ became your One sure foundation—even though you are in process, learning to rebuild your identity and secure your faith in Him in real time. The Bible says, "Nevertheless, God's solid foundation stands firm, sealed with this inscription: 'The Lord knows those who are his'" (2 Timothy 2:19).

This verse is confirmation that your salvation is irrevocable because it has been sealed into the unshakable foundation of your faith: Jesus Christ. He stands firm on your behalf, declaring you His child, despite your failures and lack of faith along the way.

When you became a Christian, as a guarantee of your salvation, God deposited His Holy Spirit within you. The Bible confirms this as well:

> And you also were included in Christ when you heard the message of truth, the gospel of your salvation. When you believed, you were marked in him with a seal, the promised Holy Spirit, who is a deposit guaranteeing our inheritance until the redemption of those who are God's possession—to the praise of his glory.
>
> ***—Ephesians 1:13–14***

As we wait for the day of salvation, the Holy Spirit continues to work within us to help us grow and mature in faith and righteousness. His presence guiding and leading us forward, and evidence of His ongoing work in our lives, is assurance God is with us, we belong to Him, and our salvation is secure. Satan claims that because we are sinful, we are unworthy to be called children of God. However, that is not the message of the gospel of Jesus Christ. The gospel of Jesus Christ says that "because of his great love for us, God, who is rich in mercy, made us alive with Christ even when we were dead in transgressions—it is by grace you have been saved" (Ephesians 2:4–5). Grace, not works! Because Jesus interceded for us to cleanse us of sin, and continues to do so, we are cleansed from all unrighteousness, sanctified, and made acceptable to receive our inheritance.

Zechariah 3 paints a beautiful picture of just what that intercession looks like for all believers in Christ:

> Then he showed me Joshua the high priest standing before the angel of the LORD, and Satan standing at his right side to accuse him. The LORD said to Satan, "The LORD rebuke you, Satan! The LORD, who has chosen

> Jerusalem, rebuke you! Is not this man a burning stick snatched from the fire?" Now Joshua was dressed in filthy clothes as he stood before the angel. The angel said to those who were standing before him, "Take off his filthy clothes." Then he said to Joshua, "See, I have taken away your sin, and I will put fine garments on you."
>
> —***Zechariah 3:1–4***

You are clothed in His righteousness, not your own. Remember, Jesus has "made perfect forever those who are being made holy" (Hebrews 10:14). This means you can take up His identity—His holiness, righteousness, and perfection—as your own. If the enemy is pointing his finger at you, trying to convince you that you will never be victorious over your sin; if he's telling you to be ashamed of yourself for your weaknesses; or if he claims that your failure to demonstrate faith over fear disqualifies you from the free gift of eternal salvation, then just point to Jesus! Recall what He did for you—how He took your place and received the punishment you deserved—and rebuke Satan in Jesus' name. Jesus removed all your guilt and shame in a single day. Yes, you are a work in progress—a so-called *burning stick snatched from the fire*—but in Christ, you are justified. You are more than enough!

As a believer, the foundation of your faith has already been laid. Now you must learn to rely on it, to trust in God's perfect love. Allow God's Word to help you discover who God really is and who you are in Him. Let it shine light into every dark corner of your heart, and drown out every voice that says you are unworthy of His love, not enough, or that you will never outrun your past. Let it remove all untruth, deception, and unbelief. Receive the Word, and you will grow to be strong and stable as the oak tree. Isaiah 61:3 says of believers in Christ,

"They will be called oaks of righteousness, a planting of the LORD for the display of his splendor."

It may be hard to conceive that one day your struggle with anxiety and fear will end or that God could one day use *you* to display His splendor. I, too, once felt this way. One day in particular, I was at home in my bedroom getting ready for the day when out of nowhere, I felt a panic attack come on. I didn't know why I was panicking, but I do remember feeling deep shame. After all this time invested and all the steps I'd gone through to overcome anxiety and fear with the help of the Lord, I thought, *How can I possibly still be struggling with anxiety and fear?*

At what point would God say enough was enough and label me a lost cause? I knew about generational curses—at least enough to know that the sins of the fathers and mothers would continue on down the family line to the third and fourth generation (see Exodus 34:7). I didn't want my children and grandchildren to struggle with anxiety and fear the way I had most of my life, but what more could I do? I felt powerless to change. Again, I cried out to God for help: *Please Lord! Maybe it's too late for me, but don't let my children suffer the way I have because of my sin.*

Desperate for a word from God, I opened my Bible and began searching for the verse about having faith the size of a mustard seed—because I figured that's about all I had in me, even on a good day. I searched but didn't find the verse I was looking for. Instead, God led me to a passage of Scripture I didn't know, and as I read it, every anxious and fearful thought instantly melted away:

> "Though the mountains be shaken and the hills be removed, yet my unfailing love for you will not be shaken nor my covenant of peace be removed," says the LORD, who has compassion on you. "Afflicted city, lashed

> by storms and not comforted, I will rebuild you with stones of turquoise, your foundations with lapis lazuli. I will make your battlements of rubies, your gates of sparkling jewels, and all your walls of precious stones. All your children will be taught by the LORD, and great will be their peace. In righteousness you will be established: Tyranny will be far from you; you will have nothing to fear. Terror will be far removed; it will not come near you. If anyone does attack you, it will not be my doing; whoever attacks you will surrender to you. See, it is I who created the blacksmith who fans the coals into flame and forges a weapon fit for its work. And it is I who have created the destroyer to wreak havoc; no weapon forged against you will prevail, and you will refute every tongue that accuses you. This is the heritage of the servants of the LORD, and this is their vindication from me," declares the LORD.
>
> —***Isaiah 54:10–17***

You see, not only was God saying that He would teach my children Himself, but they would have *great* peace. Hearing this produced an incredible sense of relief. I felt assured my children were loved by God, secure in Christ, and would not suffer for my sins as I had feared. God would lead them triumphantly forward in faith. He wasn't giving up on me either. This girl without makeup who felt anything but beautiful, with obvious flaws and imperfections, God would make beautiful with walls of sparkling jewels. He would rebuild my faith and make it strong. I would have *nothing* to fear!

Whatever the enemy has intended to use to tear you down and destroy you, rest assured, the Lord can use it to rebuild your faith and restore your life. There will be retribution, a return of all that was stolen from you or destroyed during your time of suffering. The anxiety and fear that have seemed impossible to overcome will be cast down forever. Never again will they rise to torment you. No weapon forged against you will ultimately prevail. You will soon trample the enemy under your feet!

Find your identity and security in Christ, friend. Continue taking small steps of faith with simple acts of obedience, like reading your Bible and praying every day, and God will cause your faith in Him to increase. Allow the roots of His perfect love to grow deep down into the soil of your heart, firmly establishing you upon the sure foundation of Jesus Christ, and your faith will finally begin to flourish!

You can fearlessly place all your hope in Jesus Christ. Together with Him, we are laying the groundwork for generational curses to be broken off our families and for the kingdom of God to advance in our workplaces, neighborhoods, and communities. Praise the Lord! Although people will sometimes disappoint you, your health will eventually fail, and your possessions will not last forever, a foundation of faith in Jesus Christ will stand unshakable, come what may. You can depend on the perfect love of God. My friend, at the end of the day, Jesus is all you need to secure a rock-solid faith and future.

> Therefore everyone who hears these words of mine and puts them into practice is like a wise man who built his house on the rock. The rain came down, the streams rose, and the winds blew and beat against that house; yet it did not fall, because it had its foundation on the rock.
>
> —*Matthew 7:24–25*

STEP 7:
REBUILD YOUR IDENTITY AND SECURE YOUR FAITH IN CHRIST

STUDY GUIDE

1. What masks have you been hiding behind? Is there a crutch or vice you've been relying on other than Jesus Christ—your one sure foundation?

2. Who does God say you are? Write a description of your identity in Christ, based on God's Word. Then, rehearse your identity. Here are a few verses to help get you started: John 15:15, Romans 8:37, 1 Corinthians 3:16, 2 Corinthians 5:17, Ephesians 1:4, 1 Peter 2:9, and 1 John 3:1.

3. Read Isaiah 28:16 and Luke 6:47–48. How can you establish yourself on the sure foundation of Jesus Christ, ensuring you remain free from the grip of anxiety and fear?

4. How do we become deeply rooted in God's perfect love? Read the Passion Translation of Ephesians 3:17.

5. Reread Isaiah 54:10–17. What does God promise us in this passage of Scripture? How do these promises encourage you now and give you hope for your future?

PRAYER:

Heavenly Father, Thank You for establishing me upon the sure foundation of Jesus Christ, my Rock. Thank You for Your Word, which tells me I am a child of God, an heir to the kingdom, and fearfully and wonderfully made. At times, I struggle to believe that who I am is enough. Please forgive me when I allow pride to harden my heart, preventing the seed of Your Word from taking root. I confess that, at times, I fear man's opinion more than I fear You. Father, forgive me. Help me remove any masks that keep me from being who You created me to be. Remove any barrier to Your love so I may be able to receive it, allowing its roots to grow down deep. In Jesus' name I pray, Amen.

STEP 8

PREPARE FOR PROMOTION: STAND FIRM THROUGH THE TESTING OF YOUR FAITH

Be on your guard; stand firm in the faith; be courageous; be strong.

—1 Corinthians 16:13

Seasons of severe testing and major spiritual growth often precede new opportunities to be used by God for the advancement of His kingdom. These opportunities are what I like to call a promotion. If you believe you are in a season like this, then the trials you're facing right now could be what God is using to prepare you for your promotion. Think of this promotion as a repositioning, or a leveling up, to a position of greater kingdom responsibility and spiritual authority in which you will use the testimony you carry in Christ to help others for His name's sake. We will discuss in more detail what this entails in the chapters that follow. For now, I want you to focus your attention not on the new position or repositioning that is to come, but on how you can partner with God *now* in preparing for it.

This new position or assignment will likely require you to use a greater measure of faith than you've needed to in past seasons of life. To develop the kind of faith it takes to persevere through various trials, disappointments, and suffering in pursuit of God's promises; a faith that doesn't give up or back down when confronted or opposed; one that is brave and courageous enough to fully surrender to God's will; a faith that doggedly keeps following Jesus, even when you can't see where He's leading, your faith will be tested. It's through testing and trial that we learn to stand firm in our faith rather than backslide into fear. Having rebuilt your identity and secured your faith in Christ, God now wants to ensure your faith is mature and complete, not lacking anything. In this season, you will have to learn to trust God, maybe more than you've ever had to trust Him before. As a result of your obedience to stand firm through the testing of your faith, you will grow as a true disciple of Jesus Christ—one who chooses to walk by faith, not by sight. This is the maturing process we must go through to be thoroughly equipped for the good works God has prepared in advance for us to accomplish.

One way you can know if God is preparing you for something new is when He begins to unsettle your heart, giving you a desire for life change. You will want something more, or different, you can't quite put into words but feel deep within your soul. I had this unsettling-of-the-heart experience shortly after God delivered me from the grip anxiety and fear had on my life. It became evident during the following conversation I had with my children on a car ride home from church one day:

"When I grow up, I want to be a movie maker and a scientist!" Riley exclaimed from the back seat of the car.

"I want to be an artist when I grow up!" Janie professed with great enthusiasm. "Mommy, what did you want to be when you grew up?"

My heart sank in my chest, and I took a moment to breathe out a deep, heart-heavy sigh before responding. "I never knew what I wanted to be when I grew up. There were a lot of different things I was interested in. I guess I still don't really know."

Riley, now leaning in closer to try to understand what I meant, asked, "What? Really?"

"Yes. I know I'm a teacher now, but . . ." I trailed off. I felt an overwhelming sense of deep longing for something I couldn't quite put my finger on. Caught up in emotion, choking back tears, it became impossible for me to finish my sentence. There I was, 11 years into my teaching career, seriously wrestling with a nagging, sinking feeling that there was something more I was destined to do with my life. Not that there was anything wrong with teaching. I knew God had called me into teaching to make a difference in the lives of children. I loved teaching! But deep down, I sensed there was another call on my life. Oh, how I grieved not knowing what this calling was! How I longed to feel fully alive, ignited with passion and purpose, and fulfilled in my work!

Was this a holy or unholy discontentment? Was God stirring this longing in my soul for something more, or was I simply burned out? I wasn't sure. After experiencing God's deliverance from anxiety and fear, my heart was so full of joy and love for the Lord I thought it might explode if I didn't soon find an outlet through which to release it onto others. My day-to-day life wasn't giving me the opportunity. This is how I found myself simply going through the motions day in and day out without feeling much joy or excitement for the life I was living or seeing kingdom purpose in what I was doing. The introverted and quiet side of me continued to struggle amid the busy buzz of an elementary school classroom. The stress of being a classroom teacher seemed to be compounding daily, wearing me out physically, mentally, emotionally, and spiritually. Quite simply, my human strength was fizzling out, leaving me with little left over to give to my family, friends, or anyone else. It didn't seem right. I wanted so badly to have an outlet through which I could give God glory for all He had done to rescue me. I wanted to share my story to help others struggling with anxiety and fear.

What I began to realize after the conversation with my children was that the work I was doing no longer matched the passion I felt on the inside. No matter how hard I tried to stay in line—to be the dependable wife, mom, and teacher I always had been—I couldn't reconcile the disconnect I felt between where I was and where I wanted to be. Silently, I wondered, *Will God make a way for me to share my testimony and express the love I feel for Him?* I looked for a way forward but couldn't see one. Straining to hear God's still, small voice, I pressed my ear to heaven's door.

Weeks turned into months, and I realized I was still waiting for a word from God. He had given me the faith to believe there was a new thing coming, but in the wait, I grew weary of not knowing what it was. The silence was difficult, but I learned to persevere in my work as a teacher. I knew I should maintain my current position and stand firm in my faith until God gave me a new, clear direction to move in.

Meanwhile, my husband Todd was in the midst of navigating his own possible career change. After nine years teaching high school special education, he had decided he wanted to become a police officer. One thing led to another after going out on a few ride-alongs with a close friend in law enforcement, realizing how much he loved police work, and applying for an open position with a local police department. Fast forward and Todd was nearing the end of an intense yearlong interview and background check process. It was then I sensed God saying we would need to contend for His will to be done in our family. It seemed God was calling us to a fast—for my husband's career, for my breakthrough, and for the well-being of our family as a whole. So I gathered the troops for a family meeting.

Todd, the kids, and I all committed to fast for 21 days. My kids fasted from sugar. Todd cut out meat. I stuck to a Daniel-style fast of fruit, vegetables, nuts, and seeds. Each in our own way, we prayed and fasted and stood firm in faith as a way of contending for God's will to be done in our family. On day two of the fast, Todd was officially offered a position with the police department he had applied to! God showed Himself faithful. I felt so incredibly proud of my husband and thankful to God for His blessing and provision for us! There had been six positions for several hundred applicants. Not only that, but

Todd was nearly 10 years older than the other applicants and without any kind of military training or experience. But God parted the waters for Todd to walk through. He made a way for him against all odds.

We continued on our 21-day fast. As I spent time reading God's Word, He revealed key passages of Scripture that confirmed what I sensed the Holy Spirit speaking to my heart. The reading from my daily devotional at this time was from the book of Exodus, the story of God making a way for His people Israel where there seemed to be no way. I sensed that God was telling me to persevere in faith for my breakthrough. I could almost taste it, and yet it was still just out of reach.

At this point, I desperately wanted to call it quits on teaching. In fact, I had hit a breaking point. One day stands out. It had been a particularly hard day at work. When I got home, I recall heading straight to my bedroom. I closed the door and collapsed on my bed. It was like I was comatose; I couldn't move. As I lay there, I remember thinking, *I can't do this. God, I don't see how this is your best for me or for my family.*

Then the Holy Spirit gave me a little nudge to be quiet and listen so I could hear the Lord speak. As I refocused my attention on God and released my stress to Him in that moment, I felt my heart change and my perspective shift. It seemed the Holy Spirit was at work in me, growing and strengthening my faith, leading me to declare with my next breath what I didn't have the mental or physical capacity to say a few minutes before: "Lord, if this is where you want me and what you want me to continue doing, then I will do it. I can do all things through Christ who strengthens me."

After praying, I immediately realized that God had been waiting for me to surrender *my will* for my life in exchange for *His will* for my life. This bold declaration God had me pray pushed back the enemy and refuted the lie I had been rehearsing over and over again that said, *I can't,* when in fact God had said, *Yes, you can!* This was the spiritual breakthrough I needed. The precursor in the spiritual realm to what God was planning for me in the natural world. God had been patiently waiting for me to declare His power and authority, to acknowledge who He is, and to believe that with God all things are possible!

The next morning, three days before the end of our family's 21-day fast, I awoke to the Lord saying, *Declare your breakthrough today!* In other words, God was calling me to demonstrate faith in Him by declaring my belief in His power to bring about the breakthrough I so desperately needed. Rather than a breakthrough from an internal struggle with sin and bondage as described in Step 5, this breakthrough was for an external change in my circumstances that would break open the way for me to move forward into what God was calling me to do next. Not knowing what exactly I should be expecting to see change at this point, I quickly got up and got dressed for work. Then just before heading out the door, standing firm in faith, I declared my breakthrough. Just as simple as it sounds, I said out loud, "Lord, I declare my breakthrough today!" Not in a name-it-and-claim-it sort of way, but in the way that I felt the Holy Spirit had clearly prompted me to do that morning.

I kept my spiritual eyes and ears open, watching and waiting for God to make His move. *Was all this real? Was a breakthrough truly on its way? Had I discerned the voice of God correctly?* Still doubting my strength would be enough to carry me through another crazy school day, I looked to the Lord and prayed for reassurance that He was indeed with me.

He answered me quickly. On my drive to work, God reminded me of the story of Elisha and his servant in 2 Kings, who awoke one morning to find they were surrounded on all sides by an enemy army. Overcome with fear, the servant cried out, "Oh, no, my lord! What shall we do?" (2 Kings 6:15). Elisha reassured him, saying, "Don't be afraid . . . Those who are with us are more than those who are with them" (2 Kings 6:16).

Knowing the servant still could not see or fully believe what he was saying, Elisha prayed, "'Open his eyes, LORD, so that he may see.' Then the LORD opened the servant's eyes, and he looked and saw the hills full of horses and chariots of fire all around Elisha" (2 Kings 6:17).

I knew God had brought this story to my mind to reassure me I was not alone in this spiritual battle of waiting on the Lord to discover His will for me. Like Elisha's servant, I still could not see how everything was going to work out. My breakthrough had not yet come. I was still meditating on Elisha's story on my drive to work when I heard God's voice . . . *I've got an army behind you today!*

Stunned, I almost hit the brakes in the middle of the road. *Wait, what? An angel army . . . for me, God?* Had I heard God correctly? I turned up the volume on the radio to hear what was playing, and I heard the lyrics from the song "Whom Shall I Fear [God of Angel Armies]" by Chris Tomlin come through loud and clear. I was completely blown away! The lyrics to this song confirmed I had heard God correctly. He was indeed releasing His angel army to battle the spiritual powers of darkness trying to keep me from fulfilling His plans and purposes for me! This was the confirmation I needed to stand firm while my faith was being severely tested. With renewed confidence in the Lord, sure that the promised breakthrough was indeed on its way, I arrived at school strengthened in my faith, ready for whatever opposition I would face.

Not 30 minutes into the school day, I received an email in my work inbox. I could see from the heading that it was a job posting. Intrigued, I opened the email. The posting was for an intervention resource teacher, a brand-new position. I learned that the primary responsibility of the intervention resource teacher would be to teach struggling readers in small groups, which was already a passion of mine. It was then that I realized *this* was the breakthrough I had been waiting for. God had created a way where there was no way to shift me out of the classroom position I was struggling in.

In all honesty, I was still hesitant to take the leap. I couldn't see how this move aligned with my heart's desire for ministry. This new position would stretch me in ways I wasn't sure I was ready for. It would require me to learn new things and work full time instead of part time. I wondered whether I could really do it.

Deep down, I was sure this was the direction God was calling me to move in. While the opportunity wouldn't fulfill my heart's desire to share my story, it was the next right step. This new position, while technically a lateral move, was a promotion in many respects. I would be considered a teacher leader, supporting the work the classroom teachers were doing, training teachers on new assessments and curriculum, and working closely with school administration. My reach with students would move beyond the four walls of my classroom. I would have the opportunity to work with some of the most academically and behaviorally challenged students on campus, from kindergarten through eighth grade. God was repositioning me, expanding my territory, so that I could, in turn, claim it for His kingdom! I could see that God was clearly making a way for me. Now it was up to me to walk by faith and obediently apply for the job.

The district offered me the position. I had been praying for less work, less stress, and less responsibility, but God was not going to let me settle for *less* when His desire was to bless me with more. While this position had many new responsibilities, they were all responsibilities that aligned with my gifting and came easily. They were also less physically demanding. At the end of each day, I now had energy left over for my family and friends and energy to begin exploring how God might use me to minister to others. During my time of testing, God had been working behind the scenes in ways I never imagined. He had moved people, changed hearts, and circumvented my circumstances—all to make a way for His will to be done in my life and His purposes to prevail. As my husband put it, "God chose you. He literally picked you up and planted you right where He wanted you."

God's Word defines *faith* as "confidence in what we hope for and assurance about what we do not see" (Hebrews 11:1). It takes faith to see Jesus when our faith is being tested. With hope-filled eyes of faith fixed on Jesus, though, we will witness God working and moving in ways that cannot yet be seen with our eyes of flesh, giving us a better understanding of who God is, what His will is, and what His plans and purposes are for our lives.

In Hebrews 11, also known endearingly as the *hall of faith,* we can read about bold faith being lived out in the lives of ordinary people like us, chosen by God to fulfill extraordinary callings. The stories of these ancient heroes of our faith overwhelmingly demonstrate the importance of walking by faith, not by sight (see 2 Corinthians 5:7), while waiting for the fulfillment of all God's promises. The following examples from this Bible passage will give you an idea of just what I mean:

> By faith Abel brought God a better offering than Cain did.
>
> — ***Hebrews 11:4***

> By faith Enoch was taken from this life, so that he did not experience death.
>
> — ***Hebrews 11:5***

By faith Noah, when warned about things not yet seen, in holy fear built an ark to save his family.

— ***Hebrews 11:7***

By faith Abraham, when called to go to a place he would later receive as his inheritance, obeyed and went, even though he did not know where he was going.

— ***Hebrews 11:8***

By faith even Sarah, who was past childbearing age, was enabled to bear children because she considered him faithful who had made the promise.

— ***Hebrews 11:11***

By faith Abraham, when God tested him, offered Isaac as a sacrifice. He who embraced the promises was about to sacrifice his one and only son, even though God had said to him, "It is through Isaac that your offspring will be reckoned."

— ***Hebrews 11:17–18***

By faith Moses, when he had grown up, refused to be known as the son of Pharaoh's daughter. He chose to be mistreated along with the people of God rather than to enjoy the fleeting pleasures of sin. He regarded disgrace for the sake of Christ as of greater value than the treasures of Egypt, because he was looking ahead to his reward.

—***Hebrews 11:24–26***

Like these heroes of the faith, you may need reassurance that God really is working all things together for your good, and God *is* good. When you believe something in faith that seems to contradict your present reality, or when the walls appear to be closing in and there doesn't seem to be any way out from your difficult circumstances, you can fix your eyes on Jesus, the author and perfecter of your faith (see Hebrews 12:2). If at first you cannot see Him, look again! Jesus is on the move. He is at work in your life!

Isaiah 26:3 reminds us, "[God] will keep in perfect peace those whose minds are steadfast, because they trust in [Him]." If we keep our spiritual eyes on Jesus, we will be at peace, assured of God's unfailing love and kindness toward us. As we focus our minds on Him, we will neither become distracted by chaos nor fall prey to the enemy's lies and deception. Instead, we will remain unwavering in hope, steadfast in our faith, and free from anxiety and fear. The following are a few tried-and-true practical ways you can fix your eyes on Jesus when your faith is being tested:

1. *In prayer:* The Bible tells us to "pray continually" (1 Thessalonians 5:17). Pray when you get up in the morning, when you go to bed, and every moment in between. Did you know that simply saying the name of Jesus as you breathe is a prayer that will refocus your mind back on Him? There is power in the name of Jesus. Try praying in little whispers throughout your day. Intentionally pull back from the world and spend some quiet time alone with the Lord. Share with Him all that is on your heart and mind. Don't push through feelings of anxiety, fear, and stress in your own strength; stop throughout your day to lay them at the feet of Jesus. He is there to relieve you of the weight of worry on your mind and body and to help you better understand His heart, His plans, and His purposes. The Almighty is always with you.
2. *In fasting:* Fasting, in spiritual terms, is giving up food or drink, or both, for a specific period of time for a spiritual reason. It is an expression of humility before

God and of commitment to Him. Fasting helps us to keep God the focus of our affection and attention. Just as with prayer, fasting doesn't change God; it changes us. It helps us better discern God's will and become more receptive to His plans and His purpose for our lives. Fasting also has a way of revealing our true spiritual condition, allowing us to become more aware of any deep-seated sin issues, thereby accelerating the process of moving from brokenness through repentance to transformation. If you are struggling with temptation, in need of God's divine intervention and protection, or you're waiting for a big breakthrough, fasting can strengthen your prayers and your spirit.

3. *In the Word:* Reading or listening to God's Word is one way to very literally fix your eyes on Jesus because we know from John 1:1 that Jesus is "the Word." When we meditate on and memorize *the Word*, breathing in His promises for us throughout the day, His peace will wash over us. Don't merely skim over the Word, but take the time you need to let it soak in. Slow down and seek to fully digest it. *"Taste and see that the Lord is good"* (Psalm 34:8)! You can look up Bible commentary online about particular scriptures you're drawn to. Study the historical context of the passages you're reading. Find the meaning and origin of key words to help you grasp the depth of what God is trying to unveil to you. Look for words or phrases that are repeated throughout Scripture. What might God be trying to get you to notice? Or pick a topic of interest to study and find a reading plan in your Bible app on this topic. Use Scripture, books, podcasts, and other resources to help you better understand God's Word. Allow God's

Word to transform your thoughts, renew your mind, and refocus your attention back on Him.

4. *In praise and worship:* When we praise and worship God for who He is, for all He has already done for us, and for all He is still going to do, we are choosing to look beyond what can be seen in the natural world to what can only be seen with eyes of faith fixed on Jesus. Praise and worship will stir up your faith and your beliefs, calm your heart and mind, and draw you closer to God. When we praise Him, God moves. Praise God for what He has done and what He will do. Thank Him for making a way for you! Worship Him for the greatness of His mercy and His love.

Do not be anxious or afraid. Instead, keep praying, keep fasting, keep reading the Word, and keep praising and worshiping! Wait on the Lord. God has more for you than what your eyes can see happening right now. It's in persevering through the various testing, trials, pain, and afflictions of life that our faith develops true grit and maturity and God brings about the deeper healing and restoration that our spirits, hearts, minds, and bodies need. I compare testing and trial to a surgery God performs on our hearts, always with the intention of saving us—painful as the process may be. This is also the process God often uses to prepare us for ministry—our divine callings and kingdom assignments—that are so often birthed out of our most painful experiences. In Luke 18, Jesus tells a story of why we should keep on praying and never give up.

> He said, "In a certain town there was a judge who neither feared God nor cared what people thought. And there was a widow in that town who kept coming to him with the plea, 'Grant me justice against my adversary.' For some time he refused. But finally he said to

> himself, 'Even though I don't fear God or care what people think, yet because this widow keeps bothering me, I will see that she gets justice, so that she won't eventually come and attack me!'" And the Lord said, "Listen to what the unjust judge says. And will not God bring about justice for his chosen ones, who cry out to him day and night? Will he keep putting them off? I tell you, he will see that they get justice, and quickly. However, when the Son of Man comes, will he find faith on the earth?"
>
> ***—Luke 18:2–8***

Have you been persevering in faith, but now you're struggling with severe discouragement? It's in times of severe testing, when we're pushed to the brink, that we can honest-to-goodness begin to doubt God's goodness. *Am I right?* What an energy drain discouragement is. And yet what an energy provider hope is! We all have days when it feels like our faith has run out on us, and we can't seem to muster up any more. When our faith is lacking and we can't see how our circumstances could ever change for the better, the Bible says, "Consider him who endured such opposition from sinners, so that you will not grow weary and lose heart" (Hebrews 12:3).

Are you having to wait a long time for answers? Remember the heroes of our faith who also had to wait on the Lord. Abraham waited years and years for the son God promised him. But eventually, Abraham and Sarah started to think they needed to assist God in fulfilling His promise. The bottom line: they got tired of waiting, lost faith, and fooled themselves into believing that somehow God needed their help. Sarah told Abraham to sleep with her servant so that through her servant Hagar, the family line would continue. Rather than wait on God's timing, they tried to work their own miracle.

When anxiety builds, it's not uncommon for people to try to grab the reins and take control of their circumstances. While we may feel the need to help things along, God reminds us that all He wants is our obedience and belief that He will fulfill His promises to us. Though Abraham and Sarah's faith journey was not without a few twists and turns, God fulfilled His promise to them. God blessed them with Isaac—just as He said He would.

Once we were separated from God because of our sin, but through Jesus, we were brought back into a right relationship with Him. His loving sacrifice made a way where once there was no way. So now, even when things look absolutely impossible and you can't conceive how your circumstances could ever change, remember the price Jesus paid for your freedom and complete restoration. Remember His promise to make you strong, firm, and steadfast once again (1 Peter 5:10). Then fix your eyes on Jesus and stand firm in your faith.

When we think about Jesus' crucifixion, what the cross meant to those present appeared to be utter defeat, gross humiliation, death, and finality. Now, that same cross is a symbol to all the world of hope, everlasting life, and complete victory! Your victory is not only guaranteed in Christ because of Christ—your victory *is* Christ! Jesus is your victory! He is the joy set before you, the full expression of all you've ever dared to hope and dream. He is the answer to every unanswered question. He is the Way, the Truth, and the Life (see John 14:6). Every step forward persevering in faith is one step closer to Him! Can you feel the surprising, unexpected joy of the Lord beginning to rise up within you now?

By fixing our eyes on Jesus and standing firm through the testing of our faith as we wait on the Lord, we will be empowered not only to persevere, but also to experience joy in the midst of our trials and suffering. For every bit of suffering we endure here on earth, we will be rewarded in heaven (see Matthew 5:12). This is the promise set before every believer in Christ! Knowing this promise can never be taken from us, we can laugh without fear of the future; we know the One who holds our future in the palm of His hand. Go ahead, laugh in the face of the enemy. Laugh in the face of your trials and suffering. What God has prepared for you is far greater than any of the difficulties you may be facing right now. You can trust that God is working all things together for your good. You can trust in His perfect love for you. "'For I know the plans I have for you,' declares the LORD, 'plans to prosper you and not to harm you, plans to give you hope and a future'" (Jeremiah 29:11).

Our circumstances can change in an instant. Every single day, the sun rises to expel the darkness of night. Let that sink in. Every. Single. Day. Every day, God turns the whole world around on its axis. This means that in a single day, God can turn all our darkness to light, and He can turn our whole world around! His mercies are new every morning. Never doubt the power of Almighty God to bring about the change you need to see in your life. Is anything too hard for Him?

"So we fix our eyes not on what is seen, but on what is unseen, since what is seen is temporary, but what is unseen is eternal" (2 Corinthians 4:18). In Jesus, we will have victory over every weapon forged against us and over every circumstance that attempts to exalt itself above God's sovereignty. God will redeem our stories, giving us beauty for ashes (Isaiah 61:3) and His goodness for what the enemy has meant for harm (see Genesis 50:20).

The Message translation puts it this way: "So we're not giving up. How could we! Even though on the outside it often looks like things are falling apart on us . . . There's far more here than meets the eye. The things we see now are here today, gone tomorrow. But the things we can't see now will last forever" (2 Corinthians 4:16–18 MSG). In other words, the faith and hope we have in Jesus is not a chasing after the wind. You may not be able to see it or fully grasp it yet, but you will.

The Exodus is perhaps the most well-known story in the Bible of God making a way for His people, Israel, out of what appeared to be an impossible situation. The Bible tells us that for 400 years the Egyptians enslaved the Israelites. But God remembered them and heard their cries for help.

God sent Moses to lead them out of their lives of slavery in Egypt into the land He had promised would be theirs. A land flowing with milk and honey. A beautiful, spacious land. They had finally left Egypt, full of faith and hope, only to discover that Pharaoh and his entire army were hot on their trail! The Israelites soon found themselves stuck between a rock and a hard place. Just ahead of them was the Red Sea, blocking their path to freedom. Behind them was Pharaoh's army, getting closer by the minute. There was nowhere to run.

To everyone present, their situation looked hopeless. Gripped by fear, the Israelite community began to cry out to Moses. "Was it because there were no graves in Egypt that you brought us to the desert to die? What have you done to us by bringing us out of Egypt?" (Exodus 14:11). The Israelites had all but given up hope at this point. Would their deliverance ever come?

Then Moses replied, "Do not be afraid. Stand firm and you will see the deliverance the Lord will bring you today. The Egyptians you see today you will never see again. The LORD will fight for you; you need only be still" (Exodus 14:13–14).

Then Moses raised his staff and stretched out his hand over the sea as the Lord had commanded him to do, and the water of the Red Sea began to part. With a mighty hand and outstretched arm, God drove back the sea with a strong wind, making a way for the Israelites to pass through on dry land.

Through Moses, God miraculously paved the way through the Red Sea for His chosen people, Israel, to leave their lives of slavery in Egypt for a much richer land. Just as God made a way for the Israelites to leave Egypt behind them, God will make a way for you to leave your Egypt too.

Without faith, though, hope is lost, and breakthrough is delayed. If we're not careful, the pain of our circumstances can become the loudest voice in our heads, drowning out all others—even God's voice. Our circumstances scream out things like, *You will never overcome, there's no way out of this, it's time to settle into reality and stop dreaming anything is ever going to change. Give up, already! Your faith is getting you nowhere.*

When the Israelites were overcome with fear and began to cry out, do you remember what Moses instructed them to do? He told them to *stand firm!* This is exactly what God wants us to do, too. God says, "Be on your guard; stand firm in the faith; be courageous; be strong" (1 Corinthians 16:13). What does this mean exactly? To *stand firm in the faith* is to remain resolute in your God-given convictions, immovable and unshakable in holding to your position of faith. It means to believe God is who He says He is, and God can do what He says He will do. It means to declare God's promises, while expectantly waiting for Him to move on your behalf, fully convinced that the Lord will make a way for you.

To receive the promises of God, we must believe and not doubt that we will receive what we have asked God for according to His will. If right now you're questioning whether you have the faith to believe and to stand firm, think again. The faith we need to stand firm doesn't come from us but from God. According to 2 Corinthians 1:21, "it is God who makes both us and you stand firm in Christ."

God gives us spiritual armor for the spiritual battles we must fight. In the same way that we take time to get dressed and ready for our day each morning, we also ought to take time to dress for spiritual battle. You might even decide to add this to your morning routine! Ephesians 6:13 says, "Therefore put on the full armor of God, so that when the day of evil comes, you may be able to stand your ground, and after you have done everything, to stand." We put on the full armor of God because it is what will help us stand firm in the Lord. This is an action step we can take while we wait for God to move. God's Word identifies this armor and how we are to use it:

> Stand firm then, with the belt of truth buckled around your waist, with the breastplate of righteousness in place, and with your feet fitted with the readiness that comes from the gospel of peace. In addition to all this, take up the shield of faith, with which you can extinguish all the flaming arrows of the evil one. Take the helmet of salvation and the sword of the Spirit, which is the word of God. And pray in the Spirit on all occasions with all kinds of prayers and requests. With this in mind, be alert and always keep on praying for all the Lord's people.
>
> —***Ephesians 6:14–18***

Whole books have been written on the armor of God. There is so much more that could be said here to further describe what each piece of the armor is and how to effectively use it, but instead, I'd like to remind you of how much you already know.

You may recall that in several of the steps of this book I've taught you how to use various pieces of the armor. For example, you buckled the *belt of truth* around your waist when you learned to take captive every thought and make it obedient to Christ in Step 3. In this same step, you also learned to use the *sword of the Spirit,* which is the Word of God, to replace the lies the enemy throws your way. Again, you used the *sword of the Spirit* when you reestablished your identity and secured your faith on the firm foundation of Jesus Christ and His Word in Step 7. Also in Step 7, you pulled on your *helmet of salvation* and secured your *breastplate of righteousness.* I described to you how easy it is to begin to doubt your salvation when the enemy comes to accuse you, but how Jesus rebukes the enemy and declares you righteous before Him. In Step 6, I discussed how to enter into God's presence and experience more of the *gospel of peace.* For the purposes of this chapter, I have focused mostly on utilizing your *shield of faith.*

There may be more examples you can think of from your past experiences of using different pieces of the armor of God. My hope is that this brief review of the armor we've been given helps you see how well prepared you already are to begin using it to stand firm through the testing of your faith. To learn more, I recommend checking out Priscilla Shirer's Bible study book *Armor of God* or other resources.

So when the going gets tough, remember to put on the full armor of God, fix your eyes on Jesus, and begin to boldly pray for the faith to see God's kingdom come and His will be done on earth as it is in heaven. This is no time to back down. Now is the time to trust your next big breakthrough is coming! Out of the depths of your disappointment and despair will come the still, small voice of the One who has assured you of full restoration, due recompense, and true justice.

Remember the car ride conversation with my children I shared with you at the beginning of this chapter? It was then that God's still, small voice came to me out of the depths of my own disappointment and despair, through the sweet little voice of my youngest child, Janie, to remind me of my role in His kingdom and what He had called me to do. Here's the rest of the story:

"You never knew what you wanted to be when you grew up?" Riley again inquired from the back seat of the car.

"No, I didn't," I replied. "Not really."

"Mommy," Janie gently began. "I think God is saying that you are His disciple. I hear Him saying that." Tears began welling up from within me. My daughter, then age five, continued, "Mommy, God also told me to tell you that if you want to be His disciple, you have to follow Him."

With tears now streaming down my face, I responded, "You're right, Janie! I am a disciple of Jesus. That is who I am."

Remember who you are! You, too, are a disciple of Jesus Christ if you've made Him Lord of your life. This is the highest calling one could ever aspire to. Each morning you awake with the privilege to choose to obediently follow Jesus and to believe that the Holy Spirit will lead you to all the good works God has planned and prepared in advance just for you. Simply trust God for your next steps and obediently move into position when God says, *It's time. Let's go!*

God gives us different stepping stones. When you don't know what you should do, simply trust God as far as He leads, in the moment when He leads. He may not give you the entire roadmap, but when He gives you a next step, take it. You may not be confident your next stepping stone is the right way to go yet, but rest assured, the Bible tells us, "Whether you turn to the right or to the left, your ears will hear a voice behind you, saying, 'This is the way; walk in it'" (Isaiah 30:21). Even if it seems to require more strength and faith than you think you've got in you, step out in faith in the direction you believe God is leading you.

While faith will encourage you to embrace new God-given opportunities, responsibilities, and change, fear will tempt you to shrink back, stuck in old thought processes and patterns or in positions and assignments that were never meant to last forever. Learn to persevere through the testing of your faith, standing firm till the end, and God will make a way for you to live out your purpose for His glory! He will see to it that every impossible mountain standing in your way is removed. As one of my favorite children's authors, Dr. Seuss would say, "Oh, the places you'll go! . . . Kid, you'll move mountains . . . You're off to great places! Today is your day! Your mountain is waiting. So . . . get on your way!" Mighty, faith-filled woman of God, you will soon see the new thing God has prepared for you on the other side of your obedience to follow Him!

> Consider it pure joy, my brothers and sisters, whenever you face trials of many kinds, because you know that the testing of your faith produces perseverance. Let perseverance finish its work so that you may be mature and complete, not lacking anything.
>
> —*James 1:2–4*

STEP 8:
PREPARE FOR PROMOTION: STAND FIRM THROUGH THE TESTING OF YOUR FAITH

STUDY GUIDE

1. What does it mean to fix your eyes on Jesus? Give a few practical examples of how you can do this.

2. What does it mean to stand firm in your faith? Share one or two ideas of how you can spiritually stand firm in your current circumstances.

3. As disciples of Jesus Christ, we must be willing to follow Jesus wherever He leads—even when it doesn't make sense to us, when we can't see where we are going, and when we don't know how it will work out. Are you finding it difficult to fully commit to this? If so, what would you say is holding you back?

4. With a mighty hand and an outstretched arm, the Lord will make a way for you. Read Isaiah 43:19, Exodus 14:14, Psalm 27:13–14, and Jeremiah 32:27. According to these scriptures, how can you be sure God will make a way for you to the new thing He has prepared for you?

5. When we don't yet know what we are called to do, God calls us to take the next step He's given us in faith. What do you believe God is saying is your next stepping stone?

PRAYER:

Heavenly Father, Thank You for who You are—my faithful, omnipotent God! I'm so thankful that I can trust You to work all things together for my good because You have promised to work all things for the good of all those who love You, who have been called according to Your purpose (Romans 8:28). When I cannot see You amid my circumstances, help me to remember to fix my eyes on You. When I don't know how much longer I can be strong and hold on, please give me the faith to persevere through my trials and stand firm on Your promises. When I don't know what You're calling me to do next, help me find peace and purpose in Your presence. I praise You, Jesus, that no matter where life takes me, You are the Way, the Truth, and the Life! I choose to follow You! In Jesus' name I pray, Amen.

STEP 9

LET GO OF YOUR PAST AND EMBRACE YOUR PURPOSE TODAY

Forget the former things; do not dwell on the past. See, I am doing a new thing! Now it springs up; do you not perceive it? I am making a way in the wilderness and streams in the wasteland."

—Isaiah 43:18–19

Do you know there is a calling on your life? A specific kingdom purpose God's chosen you for—"that you may declare the praises of Him who called you out of darkness into His wonderful light?" (1 Peter 2:9). Your kingdom purpose is a role only you can fulfill within the body of Christ based on how God uniquely created and gifted you. It's much more than the positive impact you can have on others in a chosen career. It's how you align yourself with the will of God, to do the good works He's called you to do, to love others to Christ and leave a lasting impact on earth for the kingdom of God. Perhaps you're longing to finally make the transition from working for what's temporal to living out your purpose for the glory of God, but there's one thing you still lack: a strong vision for who God created you to be.

You've been delivered from your Egypt, from living enslaved to fear, and God has made a way forward for you through your Red Sea—not just into a new position or assignment, but into discovering your kingdom calling, living out your God-given purpose, and fullness of life in Christ! Rather than stepping foot into your promised land, however, you've discovered, like the Israelites, God has called you to journey through the wilderness for a season. While you may feel confused by why you are now spending time in this new space, perhaps the Holy Spirit has led you into this wilderness season for a reason—that you would be thoroughly equipped for every good work the Father has prepared for you.

Fear not, friend! In your wilderness season, you may feel like you are neither here nor there, as if you took a wrong turn somewhere and got lost or off track with God, but God has not abandoned you. You may feel stuck at times, but God will be with you to show you the way through your wilderness into your promised land. In the gap between who you've been and who you're destined to become, God will further mold and shape your character. He will grow your trust in Him, make you fully dependent and reliant on Him for your every need. He will encourage you to give up your worldly desires to humbly serve Him rather than self. He will help you let go of your past (the old self) and embrace your God-given purpose (the new self) today. It's in the wilderness that God does some of His greatest work to transform us and rid our lives of anything that would come between us and Him so we can become all He's called us to be!

You may recall from the last chapter that I was "promoted" into a new teaching position within my school district. This was the way forward God clearly made for me through my own Red Sea. It's where I left behind my "Egypt" and when my wilderness season of life began. This part of my journey wasn't without many twists and turns, struggles, significant losses, heartbreaks, circling back around to lessons I thought I'd already mastered, and at times, loneliness. However, it also held exciting new life changes and opportunities to grow in my relationship with the Lord. It was a season of deep spiritual work, drawing closer to God, and learning to let go of my past to embrace my kingdom purpose and fullness of life in living for Christ.

As a teacher in the public school system, I struggled for many years not being allowed to teach openly about Jesus or share my faith. The silence was like a slow death. This may sound overly dramatic, especially since God has clearly called many Christian teachers to work in public education, but that is how it had begun to feel to me. And yet God kept me in the public schools to be a light for Him, to love and pour into the students and staff He'd surrounded me with each day. I felt a fire building inside me, but I couldn't identify what would feed it.

Not knowing where to look for pursuits that would bring more joy and fulfillment to my life, I started with what seemed most logical. I began dusting off all my old interests and passions. When painting didn't excite me, I moved on to crafting all the fun Pinterest projects I had pinned. Next, I pulled out old sheet music and sat down at my piano to play songs I'd learned as a child taking piano lessons. It wasn't that I was looking only for things that were fun and made me happy, I was looking for how my spiritual gifts and talents could be used by God in service to others to bring God glory. I needed an outlet through which to speak out, to testify to all God had done for me, share my faith, and fulfill my calling as a disciple of Jesus Christ. Surely God had a plan to release me to do His will; why the delay in revealing it to me? When would I finally know? I prayed that God would release the fire of His Spirit that felt pent up within me.

Just a few months after starting in my new position as an intervention resource teacher, I was cleaning out my desk drawers at home when I came across a tall stack of forgotten papers. As I leafed through the pages, I remembered these were journal entries from my journey overcoming anxiety and fear with the Lord. As I flipped through, I noticed the span of dates. Everything was there! The whole amazing five-year journey of my deliverance from anxiety and fear had been recorded. I stood staring at the stack of papers, thinking, *What am I going to do with all this?* Then glancing sideways at the depth of the pile, I realized, *Wow, there's enough here to make a book! Hey, maybe it is a book.*

The wheels in my head continued to spin. *Could I write a book?* Out of nowhere, a flood of ideas came rushing to my mind—a potential title, along with themes for the content of several chapters. I had never before thought of writing a book. Then I got a mental picture. It came like a flash, a vision of me speaking to a crowd on a stage inside what appeared to be a church building. Something I had never done before. I could not contain my excitement! God had revealed my passion: sharing the gospel of Jesus Christ with the world through writing and speaking! With God's help, and through my commitment to the exploration process I will describe for you below, I discovered my kingdom calling.

That fire within me was the Holy Spirit. As the prophet Jeremiah revealed about himself, so too I was feeling: "But if I say, 'I will not mention his word or speak anymore in his name,' his word is in my heart like a fire, a fire shut up in my bones. I am weary of holding it in; indeed, I cannot" (Jeremiah 20:9).

Lance Wallnau, an internationally recognized Christian speaker, business, and political strategist, advises, "When God shows you a vision, a passion, a picture of you doing something that you've never done, being somewhere you've never been, accomplishing something you've never been able to do . . . It's actually the future calling you—Answer the phone."

Your identity is ultimately in Christ as previously discussed in Step 7. However, like me, you've been uniquely created with personality, passions, and talents for the good works God has prepared just for you. The world needs your exact brand of beauty, your particular gifting and personality, the total sum of your experiences, good and bad, and the testimony you carry in Christ Jesus! This is your *kingdom calling*. Fearfully and wonderfully made, every bit of you has been created to love God and to bear the image of God to a world who desperately needs who Jesus is in you! There is only one you. You were created on purpose for a purpose only you can fulfill. I believe God will make known to you exactly what that purpose is—*for such a time as this* (see Esther 4:14).

Getting in touch with who God designed you to be is the first step in fulfilling your divine purpose, as well as your next step toward living perfectly loved. It's in discovering your purpose, your spiritual gifts and calling, that God reveals there is so much more to you than your past struggles and heartbreaks and the fears and circumstances that you thought would forever define you. Your purpose is not to serve anxiety and fear—it never was! You can develop new reactions and responses to what used to cause you anxiety and fear. You can experience joy, create new healthy habits, believe change is possible, and take up a new way of living. What held you back yesterday does not need to hold you back today. You can move forward and take possession of the good life God has for you. You have reason to hope God has a beautiful purpose for your life, and a bright future is awaiting you.

When Jesus called the Apostle Paul, then named Saul, He said to him, "Now get up and stand on your feet. I have appeared to you to appoint you as a servant and as a witness of what you have seen and will see of me" (Acts 26:16–18). This scripture gives us additional insight into what our purpose is. Like the Apostle Paul, we, too, are called to be servants of God and witnesses of what Jesus Christ has done for us. We can infer from this text that there's an urgency attached to discovering our calling and purpose. We won't discover it idly waiting for it to come to us. Our purpose is something we must pursue. While your kingdom assignments and activities may change in different seasons of life, it's important to understand your role in God's kingdom right now so you can lead others to Jesus and impact His kingdom, giving glory to God for all He has done for you. So don't delay! Discover who God is calling you to be.

If you don't yet understand your God-given purpose or how God has uniquely gifted and called you to serve Him within the body of Christ, in prayer, ask the Lord to reveal it to you. The journey to discovering your unique calling may take some time, as it did for me, but you can make the discovery process fun! It's okay to jump right on in. Don't be timid or hold back out of fear. Fear has a way of stealing the best of who we are, causing us to shrink back from outward expressions of our true selves. When fear has been removed, you will discover it's okay to be authentically you—unapologetically! You can discover the joy and freedom of living a purpose-filled life for the Lord! To begin, I suggest experimenting either with your former interests and passions or something new you've never tried. Be creative! Pray and ask God to help you with this process. God will often lead you to realize a passion that has been right under your nose all along. Ask those who know you best to offer suggestions as well. If you determine to follow God as He leads, your self-discovery journey will not lead to sin or self-indulgence. Your calling will always draw you closer to God and other people.

It may help you to consider the following questions to get you started toward self-discovery. We'll begin with some surface-level questions. Record your answers so you can reflect on them later. What makes you unique? How are you gifted and talented? How would your friends describe you? What makes you a good friend? What do you really enjoy doing?

Now, let's go a little deeper. What goals or ambitions do you have? What are you most passionate about? In what ways can your God-given gifts, talents, passions, and interests bless others? At this point, you may want to pause and consider taking an online spiritual gifts test, such as the one available for free at giftstest.com. This will help you determine what your spiritual gifts are and how God wants to use you to edify the body of Christ.

Go deeper still! Think about your testimony in Christ now. What truth, encouragement, and hope can others glean from your story that will bring glory to God? If you could do anything, what would you choose to do? What makes you feel most alive? What do you hope to accomplish in life before you die?

After thinking through your answers to all the above questions and considering your spiritual gifts, you may have realized there are things you've put on the back burner of your life you'd really like to create some margin for. Just remember, it's not necessarily what you do so much as *why* you do it that matters most. God's Word says, "Whatever you do, work at it with all your heart, as working for the Lord, not for human masters, since you know that you will receive an inheritance from the Lord as a reward. It is the Lord Christ you are serving" (Colossians 3:23–24).

To know our calling or purpose is not the ultimate goal, but to love God and to love others is. Jesus was once asked, "Teacher, which is the greatest commandment of the Law?" To which Jesus replied, "'Love the Lord your God with all your heart and with all your soul and with all your mind.' This is the first and greatest commandment. And the second is like it: 'Love your neighbor as yourself'" (Matthew 22:36–39). In our pursuit of our calling, understanding our purpose, and becoming all God's called us to be, let us never lose sight of who we are pursuing: Jesus! He is our promised land, our ultimate reward, the beginning and the end of all things. It's in Him we are perfectly loved and in Him we are found. Keep Jesus at the center of it all, pray, and God will reveal to you your divine calling. What kingdom assignment has He chosen you for?

Once you have clarity on what God is calling you to do now, you'll have one last important question to answer: *Will you say yes to the plans God has for you?*

God's plans are always better than our own. After all, this is not a journey we take down a path of our own choosing. It's not that God is becoming a part of our story, but that we are becoming a part of His story. In covenant, God said to Abram when He called him to go to a new land, "Do not be afraid, Abram. I am your shield, your very great reward" (Genesis 15:1).

The Bible tells us that Abram, whose name God later changed to Abraham, followed God in faith, even though he didn't know where God was leading him (Hebrews 11:8). If you've ever struggled with a fear of the future, fear of failure, or fear of the unknown, you may find these fears triggered again as you consider stepping out in faith. Like Abraham, it will take courage to obediently follow God—to do what you've never done and go where you've never gone—but if he can do it, so can you. As the Lord was with Abraham, God promises He will be with you.

You might be thinking, *this seems crazy! Can I even do this? God, is this really You?* Believe me, if it's from the Lord, He'll confirm it. It's okay to get clear confirmation before jumping headlong into something "crazy." God can confirm your calling through various sources, including but not limited to your spouse, family, friends, ministry leaders, His Word, a sermon, or even a literal sign. This is not to say everyone you know will agree with what you're thinking of doing and support you 100 percent. You may even have to stand alone at times in your decision to follow Christ and embrace your purpose. If you're waiting for the right timing or ideal circumstances to transition into what God is calling you to do, I'm sorry to say, there's no such thing as ideal circumstances. It's not going to get any easier to follow where God calls. You simply need to make the choice to go all in!

God is making a way forward for you through the barren, dry, desert landscape of working to survive to living a fruitful, joy-filled, purpose-driven, abundant life for Him. The way forward is not merely a promotion into a new position or assignment, but a call to discover fullness of life in Christ in loving God and loving others! 2 Corinthians 5:14 says, "For Christ's love compels us, because we are convinced that one died for all, and therefore all died. And he died for all, that those who live should no longer live for themselves but for him who died for them and was raised again."

The Lord will be faithful to fulfill His promises to you. Will you choose to obey and allow Him to continue to bless you abundantly with all He wants to give you? If you find yourself still hesitating to say yes to God, take a moment to look up the following scriptures to remember all that God has already promised you: eternal life (Romans 6:23), the forgiveness of sins (Colossians 1:14), His Holy Spirit to be with you wherever you go (Ephesians 1:13), plans to prosper you and not harm you, to give you hope, and a future (Jeremiah 29:11), to work all things together for your good according to His purpose (Romans 8:28), good works prepared in advance for you to do (Ephesians 2:10), unfailing love (Isaiah 54:10), joy (Psalm 16:11), freedom (1 Corinthians 3:17), victory (Psalm 149:4), peace (John 14:27), and everything you need for life and godliness (2 Peter 1:3).

You are in His hands. God wants you to succeed! Your kingdom call may be to scale a steep mountainside, but what you can't yet see is the escalator God's installed to help you make it to the top. He is with you to lead you every step of the way. To embrace all God is making a way for, you will have to step forward and not look back with longing for what was or what could have been. You may have to give up your plans, your hopes, and your dreams to take up *His* call. It will require you to be strong and courageous as you step out in obedience to God into an unknown future with Him. You will have to trust God's plans for you are good, and He is faithful. It won't always be easy, but I promise you it will be worth it because following Jesus always is.

When the Lord called Joshua to lead the Israelites into the Promised Land, He said: "I will give you every place where you set your foot . . . No one will be able to stand against you all the days of your life . . . Be strong and courageous. Do not be afraid; do not be discouraged, for the Lord your God will be with you wherever you go" (Joshua 1:3, 5, 9). Does the Lord not say the same thing to us today? If God has made clear your calling, you can confidently go all in knowing the Lord goes with you. There is nothing to fear.

After settling into my new teaching position, discovering my purpose, and saying yes to my call to write a book and speak for the Lord, God led me through multiple significant life transitions as part of my wilderness season and transformation journey to becoming a writer and speaker for God. While I couldn't see where I was going, I knew God was with me—even when I couldn't understand what He was doing. Some of these transitions were wonderful and filled my heart with joy and excitement, like when I started writing my book, growing in my craft, learning all the ins and outs of the industry, and connecting with other aspiring authors and speakers, agents, and publishers at writers' conferences and online.

Other transitions were extremely challenging, stretching me beyond my personal limits, causing me to rely fully on the Lord for my every need. For instance, after five years working in my new position as an intervention resource teacher, I was diagnosed with another painful chronic illness that ultimately led to my resignation from the school district I worked for. Following God's lead, I gave up my 17-year teaching career to stay home full time.

It was hard to understand why God would allow such debilitating pain and physical limitations in my life. My husband and I wondered how we would make it financially as a single-income family living in San Diego, California, one of the most expensive places in the world to live. Thankfully, God soon revealed why this was necessary and how it would work out for our ultimate good. Just a few months after I took leave, the COVID-19 pandemic hit the country, and my two school-aged children ended up home full time with me doing school via distance learning. My husband, who was serving as a police officer on the front lines during this particularly volatile time of rioting in the streets, needed my support more than ever. My time at home also gave me the opportunity to continue writing my book!

Still, other transitions broke my heart as God confirmed a need to let go and move on from a couple of close relationships. I grieved these losses especially, as they involved people I loved dearly, but I knew in order to live the life God had called me to, to remain faithful to Him rather than in emotional bondage to others, I could only move forward in the direction of His leading. I could not cling to what had been or to what I had hoped would be. I had to accept the reality that these relationships were broken. I needed to trust God to hold my heart secure and theirs through the healing process, not knowing whether or not one day these relationships might be restored.

Through each transition, God further transformed my character, increased my trust in and reliance on Him, and humbled me. He helped me embrace my worth, security, purpose, calling, and fullness of life in Christ alone. I could have let these experiences wreck me, cause me to wallow in self-pity, and grow continually in anger and bitterness. I could have let fear lead to misplaced priorities and disobedience to God, but I knew making these choices would never lead to the wholeness and fullness of life only God could give me.

Instead, I was determined to cling to God as He graciously revealed my path forward. When I felt discouraged by my circumstances or couldn't see God's hand of blessing, I held tight to His promises. I remembered Jesus' sacrifice for me, and that kept me humble and obedient. I remembered that God would not leave me in the wilderness to die (Nehemiah 9:21). He was with me and for me (Isaiah 41:10), closer than my next breath (Acts 17:28). He was leading me, like the Israelites, through the wilderness—in a cloud by day and fire by night (Exodus 13:21).

To become all God has destined for you to be as the new creation you are and to finally cross over into your personal promised land in Christ, you too will experience a type of transformation. Consider, for example, the transformation process a caterpillar undergoes to become a butterfly. After spinning a chrysalis around itself, it isn't just dormant. The caterpillar releases digestive enzymes, effectively reducing itself to nothing more than a soupy mixture of cells. It loses all semblance to a caterpillar, but all is not lost! Within that cellular soup can still be found the building blocks of an adult butterfly. Cells begin rapidly dividing and multiplying, and within two weeks, the caterpillar's transformation is complete. It can finally emerge a beautiful butterfly!

Much like the caterpillar in its chrysalis, you may experience dramatic changes. In the process of becoming a butterfly, you may feel a lack of purpose, loss of identity, and connection with the world around you. You may feel disoriented and directionless. Nevertheless, this is exactly where God wants you to be. Layers of who you have been will begin molting away, making way for new growth. Your old self—the you who may still be struggling with the pain of the past, unhelpful habits, and long-standing hang-ups—will disintegrate before your very eyes. While experiencing such significant life changes will feel quite unsettling at times, try not to see yourself as who you are in this wilderness season of transformation—which may feel a lot like broken-down butterfly soup—but as the person God has destined you to become: a beautiful woman living out the purpose for which you were created!

2 Corinthians 5:17 reminds us, "if anyone is in Christ, the new creation has come: The old has gone, the new is here!" Think of the Apostle Paul and the amazing transformation he went through. As you may recall, he became as passionate about spreading the Gospel message and reconciling people to Christ as he once was about killing Christ's followers. Talk about a dramatic transformation! Paul went through a period of blindness after meeting God face-to-face on the road to Damascus (Acts 9:1–19), where he literally could not see anything, much less understand his purpose. It wasn't until Paul accepted Christ and became a new creation in Him that God removed the scales from Paul's eyes so Paul could see again physically, as well as see he had been living his life all wrong and had misunderstood his purpose. He needed to be dramatically transformed, and only God could do it.

To take up the new self in Christ and move forward with your life, you will need to break up with anything still keeping you tied to your old self. It's time to finally let go of your past. The Bible confirms this, saying, "everything—and I do mean everything—connected with that old way of life has to go. It's rotten through and through. Get rid of it! (Ephesians 4:20–24 MSG)." This could include sinful desires, unhelpful habits, hang-ups, unhealthy ways of thinking, toxic relationships, and positions and assignments that are no longer relevant to your life in Christ now.

Matters of the heart, such as doubt, insecurity, shame, grief, anger, regret, resentment, bitterness, pride, envy, comparison, anything that distracts you from your purpose and keeps you in emotional bondage, tied or indebted to anything other than Christ, or takes your focus off God, must go. The fears you've overcome are a part of your past now or what would be considered the old self. You are no longer bound to serve fear or anything that would bind you to it. Remember, your allegiance is to Christ! You have decided to fear the Lord your God above all else and to serve Him only, rather than self and the things of this world.

Consecrate means to separate yourself from the things that would make you unclean, especially anything that might contaminate your relationship with a perfect God. The Israelites had to consecrate themselves by washing and purifying themselves from their physical and spiritual uncleanness to devote themselves wholly to the Lord. Only then would He open up the way for them to cross over into the Promised Land (see Joshua 3:5).

While we have already been washed by the blood of Jesus and made clean by His death and resurrection, God still calls us to consecrate ourselves through repentance by regularly confessing our sins to purify our hearts. And rather than conforming to the patterns of this world and living for ourselves, instead God calls us to consecrate ourselves by offering our bodies as living sacrifices to Him in total devotion.

Thus, a part of your transformation into who God called you to be will include a time of sanctification or what I have called letting go of your past. God will begin uncovering and revealing to you any space in your heart that is not yet fully surrendered to Him. With His help, you can rid your life of any attitudes, thoughts, and behaviors that keep you from growing in obedience to Him.

For example, you might notice you have become legalistic—putting heavy, unrealistic expectations on yourself. For goodness' sake, drop those heavy chains! We are justified by our faith in Jesus Christ, not on the basis of our works. Ephesians 2:8 reminds us, "For it is by grace you have been saved, through faith—and this is not from yourselves, it is the gift of God—not by works, so that no one can boast."

Are you experiencing tension in some of your personal relationships? Is it possible you're growing apart? If so, allow them, and yourself, the freedom to make adjustments as needed. Be gracious and tender-hearted with the people in your life while they try to make sense of your changing relationship. Either your relationship will grow with the changes and you'll find new understanding for each other and ways of connecting, or you'll end up going your separate ways. It may be time for you to move on if the reason or season for your friendship has passed.

Note: This should not be misinterpreted as marriage advice. Please understand that I'm not suggesting walking away from a marriage relationship here. That's a topic for an entirely different book. If you're struggling in your marriage relationship, I recommend you seek help from a professional therapist or pastor you can trust.

Is there someone you need to forgive? Let go of the record of wrongs done to you and allow the perfect love of God to heal your broken heart. When we rehearse the pain of the past over and over again in our minds, the pain robs us of experiencing joy and peace in the present. Our past need not hold us captive or define our future.

God can sanctify us from being so comfortable that we become stagnant, no longer willing to go out of our way to help others, grow spiritually, or share the gospel of Jesus Christ. This new season of transformation will encourage you to step out with boldness and courage and try something new. Look for opportunities and be willing to embrace what God makes a way for.

Carefully consider what you give your time and energy to. Even things you consider *good* may not be God's best for you. As people who are set apart for God, we must maintain boundaries in obedience to God—we must guard our hearts and minds in Christ Jesus. In maintaining physical, spiritual, and emotional boundaries with others and with ourselves (self-discipline), for our good and the good of others, we will mature. We will experience more joy and freedom. We will be ready to be used by God to do the good works He's prepared for us!

There are many good things that can occupy your time and keep you from doing what's most important or best. For example, when God asked me to write this book, I had what I considered nonnegotiables with how I spent my time and energy. God made it clear that everything is negotiable. For a season of growth and learning, I had to clear my schedule. I gave up other impactful ministries I was involved in, important social gatherings with family and friends, and more. This was difficult for me, given that my love language is quality time, and these people are very special to me. But during this time of letting go and surrendering one thing after the next, God made it clear to me—*He knows what is truly best.*

Listen to what God is calling you to do and follow Him. Ultimately, your relationship with the Lord and the condition of your heart are what matter most! God will not leave you empty-handed. He will draw you closer and reveal more of Himself to you—more of His glory! You will learn to cling to Him rather than the world and bask in the fullness of who He is. The Apostle Paul explains this perspective shift we can take up as followers of Jesus: "What is more, I consider everything a loss because of the surpassing worth of knowing Christ Jesus my Lord, for whose sake I have lost all things. I consider them garbage, that I may gain Christ and be found in him" (Philippians 3:8–9).

God will fill your life with good things. Trust Him when He says it's time to let go of your plans or whatever else He is asking you to release to Him. It means He's got something better He wants to give you! It isn't about perfection, which is not possible for us to attain. Our imperfections do not get in the way of God using us to minister to others. God can use us at any time, even as we are working out our sin with Him. Isn't that amazing? It's about becoming aware of what's holding us back from making progress and doing the work with the Lord to remove anything that hinders His message or makes it difficult for us to love God and love others.

You can't harvest tomorrow's field with one foot still planted in yesterday's soil. Holding on and staying put when the Lord is telling you, *It's time to let go and move on*, you'll wind up stuck, spiritually speaking, caught in a never-ending loop circling your wilderness. Your faith may atrophy, increasing your risk of becoming depressed, disillusioned, or bitter in life. Holding back from your purpose, you'll miss out on the abundant life God wants you to experience. There may still be lingering pain or deep-rooted sin you need to work through with the Lord before crossing over into your promised land. Now is the time to finally let go of the record of wrongs done to you and allow the perfect love of God to heal your broken heart. Cut ties with anything that keeps you bound to your old, dead self. Draw that proverbial line in the sand and leave the past where it belongs—in the past!

We have already learned that there is power in the blood of Jesus. As believers, we stand now under the protection of His blood. Which means, although we usually won't forget painful experiences, the blood of Jesus frees us from their power over us. In other words, the memory may remain, but the pain will be gone. As a child of God, then, you can declare that what is "under the blood" cannot step foot into your present or future! Leave behind what you've previously let define you and walk into the destiny God has planned for you. We can embrace all God's Word says in Philippians 3:13: "Brothers and sisters, I do not consider myself yet to have taken hold of it. But one thing I do: Forgetting what is behind and straining toward what is ahead" (Philippians 3:13). Amen!

For everything, there is a season. Yes, the Lord gives, and the Lord takes away. God is so gracious and patient with us, though. He lovingly tells us, *Let go of who you were and embrace all of who you're destined to become. Draw near to Me, and you will see that I've got more for you. Come, follow Me.*

After ridding your life of the old self, Ephesians tells us to "then take on an entirely new way of life—a God-fashioned life, a life renewed from the inside and working itself into your conduct as God accurately reproduces his character in you" (Ephesians 4:20–24 MSG). By cooperating with the Holy Spirit and allowing God to change you from the inside out, you are daily being transformed into Christlikeness! We can look back with longing toward the past, or we can get excited about the privilege of partnering with God in all He has planned—more than all we could think to ask for or imagine (Ephesians 3:20).

Like the Apostle Paul, and so many other men and women of faith who have gone before us, God will continue to mold and shape us, helping us to become the new creation He's called us to be. However, if we aren't careful to obey the Lord's leading, our time in the wilderness may take longer than we would like it to. The Israelites spent 40 years circling the desert in transition between Egypt and the Promised Land after God banned them from entry because they doubted God's power to give them victory over the Canaanites who inhabited the land. Their transition took much longer than they ever imagined it would! Unfortunately, in the wait and in the fear of the unknown, many of the Israelites lost hope of entering the Promised Land. In fact, the generation that originally left Egypt died before ever getting there. Because of their lack of faith and disobedience, it was their children whom the Lord led to cross the Jordan River to take possession of the Promised Land.

Like us, God's chosen people, the Israelites, had a choice to make: to trust God with His plan for their lives, to follow Him wholeheartedly, to be strong and courageous, and to cross the Jordan River in faith—or to settle in the desert and always wonder what could have been. To stop following after God and settle in the desert instead was tempting. The desert was barren, but it was familiar, relatively safe, and predictable. To cross the Jordan and enter into the Promised Land came with risk from a worldly perspective.

Like the Israelites, we will be tested by God during seasons of transition; this is one way God tests our commitment to trust and obey Him. Did you know even Jesus' commitment was tested for 40 days and nights in the desert before He began His ministry here on earth? The Bible tells us:

> Jesus was led by the Spirit into the wilderness to be tempted by the devil. After fasting forty days and forty nights, he was hungry. The tempter came to him and said, "If you are the Son of God, tell these stones to become bread." Jesus answered, "It is written: 'Man shall not live on bread alone, but on every word that comes

> from the mouth of God.'" Then the devil took him to the holy city and had him stand on the highest point of the temple. "If you are the Son of God," he said, "throw yourself down. For it is written: 'He will command his angels concerning you, and they will lift you up in their hands, so that you will not strike your foot against a stone.'" Jesus answered him, "It is also written: 'Do not put the Lord your God to the test.'" Again, the devil took him to a very high mountain and showed him all the kingdoms of the world and their splendor. "All this I will give you," he said, "if you will bow down and worship me." Jesus said to him, "Away from me, Satan! For it is written: 'Worship the Lord your God, and serve him only.'"
>
> —*Matthew* ***4:1–10***

Satan tempted Jesus when He was presumably at His weakest—physically, mentally, and emotionally. Unlike the Israelites and us, Jesus never succumbed to temptation. He would not trade the promises of God for the temporary pleasures of this world. He trusted God the Father to be faithful to fulfill His promises. His only desire was to accomplish the will of His Father. Jesus stood upon the Word of God, and Satan had to flee. It was after those 40 days in the desert, having withstood temptation, that Jesus was released to begin His ministry.

While it may be tempting to settle for what the world has to offer and succumb to the desires of the flesh, it will not be God's best for you. The Bible warns us in 1 John 2:15–17: "Do not love the world or anything in the world. If anyone loves the world, love for the Father is not in them. For everything in the world—the lust of the flesh, the lust of the eyes, and the pride of life—comes not from the Father but from the world. The world and its desires pass away, but whoever does the will of God lives forever."

Transformation is not typically a quick process. When we look to some of our favorite men and women of faith in the Bible, we find that they too had to wait a long time. Joseph waited 13 years, from the time he was 17 years old tending flocks until he was 30, before he entered the service of Pharaoh, king of Egypt (Genesis 37:2; Genesis 41:46). Abraham waited 25 years from the time God first promised to make him a "father of many nations," until his wife Sarah gave birth to Isaac (Genesis 17). Moses waited 40 years, wandering through the desert with an unbelieving generation of Israelites before they reached the land God had promised to give the Israelites. Moses never got to enter the Promised Land himself, but he did receive God's promise of eternal salvation (Genesis 3:7–8; Joshua 3). And finally, Jesus waited 30 years to begin His ministry (Luke 3:23). Unfortunately, we can't hurry this process. Only God knows the time that is needed to prepare you to move forward into your purpose.

Remember, the Holy Spirit has led you into your wilderness season for a reason—so you would be thoroughly equipped for every good work the Father has prepared for you. Be patient with yourself. Your time in transition is not about perfection, but about letting His perfect love transform you so that you can, in turn, transform the world with His perfect love! It's about coming into a deeper understanding of who Jesus Christ is in you and becoming more Christlike because Christ in you is just who this world needs (see Philippians 3:8; 1 John 4:17)!

Maybe you think that it's too late for you, though. You've told yourself, *I've wandered for too long in the desert, given into temptation far too many times, and disqualified myself from the prize.* But Jesus took up our imperfections and canceled our debt. Who you are now is who Christ is in you. So let your past go. His promises are for you! The Bible says, "For God's gifts and his call are irrevocable" (Romans 11:29). While you may feel a great deal of uncertainty about what your future holds, you can have absolute certainty in the One who holds your future. The Lord will be with you to help you conquer the giants in the land and take down the walls that stand in your way.

God wants you to see that a new day is dawning. Change is now peering over the horizon of your life. God says, "Forget the former things; do not dwell on the past. See, I am doing a new thing! Now it springs up; do you not perceive it? I am making a way in the wilderness and streams in the wasteland" (Isaiah 43:18–19). God did not do a complete renovation of your life to seemingly leave you in the same place you've been. God is not in the business of closed doors and dead ends or of a sunset without a sunrise. God will always make a way through your darkest days and deepest pain into His land of promise.

Right now, you are exactly where you need to be—in the midst of being prepared and equipped for God's call on your life, waiting for Him to open a way for you to cross over into the future He has for you. Rest in Him while you wait. Surrender to Him. God can do all He has promised—not because of who you are, but because of who He is in you. His grace will sustain you. God sees your future, He knows your past, and He is well aware of your present weaknesses, vulnerabilities, and abilities too. Sure, you may have to circle the desert a few times, but He'll get you to the water's edge. And when He says it's time, you will be ready. He will part the waters, and you will cross confidently over into your promised land.

See, the Lord your God has given you the land. Go up and take possession of it as the Lord, the God of your ancestors, told you. Do not be afraid; do not be discouraged.

—*Deuteronomy* ***1:21***

STEP 9:
LET GO OF YOUR PAST AND EMBRACE YOUR PURPOSE TODAY

STUDY GUIDE

1. Exploring ways to use your passions, gifts, and talents to further the kingdom of God can be a fun process! If you could try something new, what would it be?

2. Given your experiences and testimony in Jesus Christ, particular interests, spiritual gifts, skills, and passions, how is God calling you to share the hope and love of Jesus Christ with the world? Whom is He calling you to minister to? Consider what opportunities He has given you to make a difference right where He has planted you.

3. Read 1 John 2:15–17. What three worldly temptations does Satan use to distract us and tempt us to sin? What sort of temptations do you find yourself most vulnerable or susceptible to? Read Luke 4:1–13. What defense strategy did Jesus use to keep from falling prey to temptation, and how can you incorporate this strategy for yourself?

4. Is there anything dividing your devotion to God that you sense God calling you to let go of now, or is there anything keeping you from embracing your purpose that you need to consecrate to Him? (Hint: Does anything or anyone spe-

cific immediately come to mind when you think about the following: unforgiveness, resentment, bitterness, doubt, fear, shame, or insecurity? Does holding on to this person or thing move you toward Christ and forward in His will for your life, or does it exalt your past and hold you back from embracing your purpose and fullness of life in Christ?)

5. It takes tremendous courage to let your past go to do what you've never done, go where you've never gone, and be who you've never been. Is there something that God is calling you to say *yes* to? If so, what next step of obedience could you take to keep yourself moving in the direction of becoming who God called you to be?

PRAYER:

Heavenly Father, Thank You for leading me through the unfamiliar territory of the wilderness I now find myself in. Please use this time to teach, refine, mold, and shape me into who You've called me to be. Give me a vision for my future. Show me my purpose and what next steps of obedience I can take to embrace it and fulfill my kingdom calling. Father, give me also the strength and wisdom to know how to battle temptation in this desert place. And when it's time for me to cross over into my promised land, Father, supply me with the courage I need to leave the pain and sins of my past in the past. In Jesus' name I pray, Amen.

PART III:
THE RELEASE

Then I heard the voice of the Lord
saying, "Whom shall I send? And
who will go for us?" And I said,
"Here am I. Send me!"

—Isaiah 6:8

STEP 10

LET YOUR LIGHT SHINE BY HELPING OTHERS

In the same way, let your light shine before others, that they may see your good deeds and glorify your Father in heaven.

—Matthew 5:16

Friend, if I could reach through these pages right now, I'd give you a big hug and tell you just how proud of you I am! As painful and challenging a process as it's likely been to work through each of the steps to overcome your anxieties and fears, you've kept going, persevering in your faith! And now God, who rescued you out of the darkness and restored you, is going to release you to draw others toward the light of His perfect love. It's time to rise, to shine, using the gifts God has given you and your testimony to share love and hope with those living in darkness and to light the way to salvation in Jesus Christ. In other words, "Your mission is to live as children flooded with his revelation-light! And the supernatural fruits of his light will be seen in you—goodness, righteousness, and truth" (Ephesians 5:8–9 TPT).

Do you recall how afraid I used to be to pray aloud in front of anyone? After uncovering the root cause of this fear and making progress through the steps God used to rescue and restore me, God gave me another opportunity to confront that fear. My phone rang. It was my pastor, calling to ask me if I would pray onstage over the congregation for both Sunday services. It was the start of the new year, and our church was about to begin a corporate 40-day fast, and the members would commit to read through the entire Bible in one year. My pastor specifically asked me to "pray Heaven to Earth." Good grief! No pressure.

I wanted to break it to him gently that I was not the right person for this job, but I managed to refrain from doing so. While I was both honored and humbled he had asked me, I wasn't sure I fit the profile of the person he was looking for. I was not a bold, dynamic speaker, but rather soft-spoken, insecure, and easily intimidated by large crowds.

To get up on stage and pray at the Sunday services in front of hundreds, maybe thousands, of people was certainly not in my comfort zone. Just thinking about doing so, I felt my palms get sweaty and my heart rate go up. My flesh screamed *no!*

Despite my insecurities and trepidation, deep down I knew God had already been speaking to my heart about being bold and brave and stepping outside of my comfort zone—and this was an opportunity to trust Him. This was a test of my obedience to do what He was calling me to do: to help others regardless of whether I felt qualified and in spite of whatever fears I was still learning to work through. He wanted me to let my light shine!

I couldn't deny there was a big part of me that really wanted to go for it! From somewhere deep within, an emphatic resounding *yes* was desperately trying to make its way out of my mouth and into my pastor's ear. The Holy Spirit urged me to go for it! I wanted to be faithful. I didn't want to cower in fear and insecurity at the opportunity and say like Moses, *Please send someone else* (Exodus 4:13).

This prayer wasn't about me anyway. It was about encouraging my church family, praying God's blessing over them for the coming year and humbling myself in service to the body of Christ. God would be faithful to give me the words He wanted me to pray over them and to Him. So after much deliberation during our brief five-minute phone conversation, I finally said yes and committed myself. Even if it meant doing it afraid, I was not going to let this opportunity pass me by.

The truth is, God doesn't always call the most eloquent orators to be a voice for Him. It's often the most unlikely of people who shine His light. Take Moses, for example. The Bible says in Exodus 3 that Moses was out tending to his father-in-law's flocks when the Lord called him.

On Mount Horeb (the mountain of God), "the angel of the LORD appeared to him in flames of fire from within a bush. Moses saw that though the bush was on fire it did not burn up" (Exodus 3:2). The Lord said to Moses, "'I have indeed seen the misery of my people in Egypt . . . I am concerned about their suffering. So I have come down to rescue them . . . So now, go. I am sending you'" (Exodus 3:7, 8, 10).

God called on Moses to help deliver His people out of slavery. However, Moses was very much afraid and insecure. Bottom line? He felt unqualified for what God was calling him to do. Rather than humbly obeying God, Moses was reluctant to comply. He questioned God's plans, argued with Him, and essentially declared himself unfit for the job. He said, "Who am I that I should go to Pharaoh . . ." (Exodus 3:11) and "I have never been eloquent . . . I am slow of speech and tongue" (Exodus 4:10).

At this point, Moses is unable to move past his insecurities and fears, and he is looking for a way out of his God-given assignment. He sees what God is asking him to do only in terms of his limitations rather than seeing what God can do in and through him! Fully knowing Moses' weaknesses, God patiently waited for him to come around to obedience. He gently responded to Moses' insecurities and fears with a variety of assurances, miraculous signs, and wonders. He said, "I will be with you" (Exodus 3:12) and "I will help you" (Exodus 4:12).

Rather than accept God's reassurances, though, Moses questioned God, further revealing his insecurity, fears, and doubts. "Suppose I go to the Israelites and say to them, 'The God of your fathers has sent me to you,' and they ask me, 'What is his name?' Then what shall I tell them?" (Exodus

3:13). Unfortunately, Moses still doesn't get it. He isn't ready to grasp the fullness of who God is.

God answered Moses, "'I AM WHO I AM. This is what you are to say to the Israelites: 'I AM has sent me to you'" (Exodus 3:14). Mic drop.

I want you to understand the power and weight of this statement. *I AM* is the name God gives to Himself, as first revealed to Moses. This name is all-encompassing, describing God's presence, sovereignty, sustainability, and power over all; our God who was, who is, and who is to come. By God calling himself *I AM*, He was essentially revealing to Moses the fullness of who He is. Whatever it was the Israelites lacked—or that Moses lacked—*I AM* would be for them. The leaders of the Israelites would have grasped the significance of this declaration and been in awe. In God referring to himself as *I AM*, I believe it's as if God was saying to Moses: *I know who I AM, but do you know who I AM? I know who you are, but do you know who I AM in you?*

It's worth noting that God's name is transcribed as YHWH, or Yahweh, in the original Hebrew Old Testament. This is because the Jews believed God's name was too sacred to be uttered out loud and therefore had to find substitutions for it. Since there is not an exact translation in the English language for Yahweh, we usually find God's name written as "LORD" in all capital letters in our English Bibles. These different forms of God's name all refer back to *I AM.*

Like Moses, we have been called to lead people into the promised land of eternal salvation in Jesus Christ! We are people on a mission, sent to declare the praises of Him who called us out of darkness into His wonderful light (see 1 Peter 2:9). We can fight, flail, get anxious, angry, and argue with God about what He's calling us to do. We can doubt ourselves or see ourselves as unqualified for the opportunities God gives us to help others. Or we can take our eyes off ourselves and see God—looking to all that *I AM* is, rather than fearing all that *I am* not:

I AM your Deliverer (Psalm 140:7).
I AM your Strength (Psalm 28:7).
I AM your Righteousness (Isaiah 61:10).
I AM your Light (Psalm 27:1).
I AM your Shepherd (John 10:11).
I AM your Provider (Genesis 22:14).
I AM your Defender (Proverbs 23:11).
I AM the Way, the Truth, and the Life (John 14:6).
I AM everything that you need (2 Corinthians 9:8)!

With Christ in you and you in Him, you will shine bright in this world! Not because of who you are, but because of who He is in you. Christ within you is like the fire inside the burning bush—His presence turns you into a soul burning with a passion to see God's kingdom come and His will done on earth as it is in heaven (see Matthew 6:10). Just as the fire within the bush did not burn out, so the fire of the Holy Spirit within you will never be extinguished. So never be afraid to let your light shine. No matter what God has called you to, He will be with you.

In Ezekiel 47, we read about a vision Ezekiel had of a river flowing from the house of God into the sea. This river was said to have fresh water flowing through it, making the salt water fresh so that where the river flowed everything lived. On both sides of the banks of the river, fruit trees grew. About these fruit trees, the Bible says, "Their leaves will not wither, nor will their fruit fail. Every month they will bear fruit, because the water from the sanctuary flows to them. Their fruit will serve for food and their leaves for healing" (Ezekiel 47:12).

So what do these fruit trees represent? They're Christians! Jesus said, "Whoever believes in me, as Scripture has said, rivers of living water will flow from within them" (John 7:38). As we stay connected to the source of life, Jesus, His living water will continue to flow down to us and pour out through us, providing nourishment and healing to those who will receive it. The flow of this river will not ebb away. Rather, its flow will continue to grow stronger. With the measure we use, it will continue to be measured to us (see Matthew 7:7). We will be as the Bible describes the trees on either side of the banks of the river, whose leaves do not wither and who never fail to bear fruit.

As Christians, we are to be known by our fruit. The Bible describes fruit in terms of the Spirit: "love, joy, peace, patience, kindness, goodness, faithfulness, gentleness, and self-control" (Galatians 5:22–23). This is the good that comes out of us because the Spirit of God, or Holy Spirit, is working in us and shining through us. Jesus said, "You did not choose me, but I chose you and appointed you so that you might go and bear fruit—fruit that will last—and so that whatever you ask in my name the Father will give you" (John 15:16).

How it works is this: we act in love out of the overflow of God's perfect love for us, and our actions help others see the light of God's love! They will see Jesus in us and be drawn to Him! But how do we let our light shine and glorify God with our actions? First, we can bring glory to God by living holy and righteous lives. Others will see and admire your obedience to God. We want to become the kind of people who can be trusted to do what is right—even when no one is looking.

Next, we can glorify God by allowing our hearts to be filled with love and compassion for the hurting and broken. Like the Good Samaritan (see Luke 10:25–37), when we see someone who is down-and-out or needs help, we shouldn't just carry on and ignore them. If it's safe to do so, we should stop to lend a helping hand. We should go out of our way to satisfy a need that they have. We become the answer to their prayers! This doesn't mean you are required to solve all their life's problems or to meet their every need. Simply do whatever you are cheerfully willing to do or whatever God lays on your heart. Whether big or small, your gesture will show that God sees them and that He loves and cares for them deeply. A little bit of courage and kindness can go a long way.

We can also glorify God by using the gifts He's given us to bless others. We are blessed to be a blessing. Ask yourself, what has God gifted me with (time, talents, money, etc.) that I can give to someone else? The key is to use what you have been given and pay it forward!

Additionally, we can bring glory to God through our praise and worship of Him. Your praise and worship—whether it's in a song you sing or the words you speak to and about God—send the message that true love, joy, and peace is found only in relationship with Jesus Christ. This encourages and emboldens others to seek out a relationship with Jesus for themselves.

Finally, you can glorify God by sharing your testimony. By telling others what God has done for you, they will see the transforming power of God. When they see how God has changed your life for the better, it will give them hope that God can do the same for them. Continue to let your light shine by helping others, and the Holy Spirit will lead you to those in need—to those whose lives will be changed because of the beautiful light and love of Christ in you.

The Lord has also revealed to us some of the ways in which we can put our faith into action and let our light shine. He said, "Is not this the kind of fasting I have chosen: to loose the chains of injustice and untie the cords of the yoke, to set the oppressed free and break every yoke? Is it not to share your food with the hungry and to provide the poor wanderer with shelter—when you see the naked, to clothe them, and not to turn away from your own flesh and blood?" (Isaiah 58:6–7).

When people see the glory of God in you, through your loving acts of kindness, in the nice things you say and do, and in how you live your life for Jesus, the perfect love of God becomes manifest in you and given out through you. You will find fullness of joy and wholeness in living for the cause of Christ rather than living controlled by fear. You will see the glory of God! The Bible also says that in choosing to minister to the hurting, the lost, and the broken—even in times when you, yourself, may be struggling—you will be rewarded: "Then your light will break forth like the dawn, and your healing will quickly appear; then your righteousness will go before you, and the glory of the Lord will be your rear guard. Then you will call, and the Lord will answer; you will cry for help, and he will say: Here am I" (Isaiah 58:8–9).

We will not always get to see the fruit of all our efforts to love and serve others, though. For example, you may be in a position where you feel you have limited opportunity to openly share the gospel, and you may wonder if you are making any kind of difference at all. Does that mean you should give up? No way! When we cannot see the fruit of our labor of love in the Lord, the Bible encourages, "Let us not become weary in doing good, for at the proper time we will reap a harvest if we do not give up. Therefore, as we have opportunity, let us do good to all people, especially to those who belong to the family of believers" (Galatians 6:9–10).

In other words, we are to continue to be humble, obedient servants by showing up and making ourselves available to whatever God wants to do in and through us, trusting there will be a harvest whether or not we personally get to see and experience it. Ultimately, we are not responsible for another sinner's salvation. That's God's department. His promise to us is simply this: that if we remain in Him, we will "bear much fruit" (John 15:5).

My prayer for you, then, is "that our God may make you worthy of his calling, and that by his power he may bring to fruition your every desire for goodness and your every deed prompted by faith" (2 Thessalonians 1:11).

When it's almost harvest time and the fruit of your labor is ripe for the picking, however, beware! The enemy of your soul will try to kill, steal, and destroy the seeds of truth and love that you have been diligently planting and watering. Be strong in the Lord when He comes to attack so you don't fall prey to a fear of failure. Satan will try to deceive you into believing your work in the Lord has been for naught, minimize your impact in this world for God's kingdom, and convince you that you have miserably failed to accomplish the very things God has called you to do. Don't let the enemy distract you from this truth: you are the light of the world!

As a disciple of Jesus Christ, you have been chosen for such a time as this. The world needs to know Jesus! He is coming soon! The Bible says that before Jesus Christ returns, the dark is going to get darker, and evil will increase on the earth (see Acts 2:20; Matthew 24:12). However, because Jesus shines through you, you can be the light that those walking around in darkness need to see to understand *Who* hope is—to finally recognize the Light of the World who came down to earth for them all those years ago!

Remember the year 2020? Who doesn't? In the midst of the worldwide COVID-19 pandemic, one of the darkest times in recent human history, many were struggling with panic, anxiety, and fear like never before. Everything shut down—restaurants, salons, businesses, schools, churches. We were forced to live six feet apart from friends and neighbors and to cover our faces with masks. For many, their faith was tested like never before. It was a year of violent protests in the streets and political unrest. Lives were turned upside down. Brother turned against brother. Many people picked up their families and moved to places they had never before imagined living. People lost jobs, resigned from jobs, and started homeschooling their children. There was no sense of normalcy and predictability. Greatly perplexed and distressed, all were left wondering, *Can light still be seen here on earth?*

Then on December 21, 2020, literally the darkest day of the year, a bright light shone into the darkness! Jupiter and Saturn aligned with each other for the first time since 1226! Their convergence made them appear as though they were touching—two heavenly bodies reflecting the light of the sun, coming together for us, to increase light and hope for those living in darkness. This once-in-a-lifetime event reminded me of the Bethlehem star that shone on the day Jesus, the Light of the World, came down for us. I believe this was a heavenly sign to say *Yes, light can still be seen in the world!*

Whether you were personally a witness to this event and aware of its occurrence or not, aren't we just like these celestial bodies in a way? Each of us believers in Christ, a heavenly body created to reflect the light of the Son into a world in need? How much brighter the light of Jesus shines within us when we come together in love and share our light with others. Time and again, I've been met with unexpected blessings when I reach out in love to help others. How beautiful and fulfilling it is to let your light pierce the darkness in someone else's life, making space for love to grow.

How do we reveal the light of Jesus to a world in need without becoming overwhelmed by the darkness that surrounds? Matthew 6:22 says, "The eye is the lamp of the body. If your eyes are healthy, your whole body will be full of light."

Therefore, to become full of God's revelation-light—so full that it spills out into the darkness that surrounds—we must keep our eyes on God! We do this by spending time in God's Word and in His presence.

In the Psalms, David wrote about how the Word will fill us, saying, "The unfolding of your words gives light; it gives understanding to the simple" (Psalm 119:130) and "Your word is a lamp for my feet, a light on my path" (Psalm 119:105). Likewise, 1 John 1:5 reveals the importance of spending time in God's presence to receive more of His revelation-light, saying, "God is light. In Him, there is no darkness at all." As we spend consistent time in God's presence, we will be continually filled with the light of God's love.

Another key way we can avoid becoming overwhelmed by the evil in the world is to "overcome evil with good" (Romans 12:21). While Satan would like nothing more than for you to shrink back and hide your light, you can refuse to bow to fear and shine your light anyway. In fact, God calls us to this in His Word, saying, "But you are a chosen people, a royal priesthood, a holy nation, God's special possession, that you may declare the praises of him who called you out of darkness into his wonderful light" (1 Peter 2:9). This is how you push back against the evil that abounds. It's how God is glorified! Jesus gives us His glory—the glory the Father gave to Him—so that we, in turn, can reveal Jesus to the world.

A light that is hidden or refuses to shine, does no good. It's of no use. So, be intentional about letting your light shine because the actions we take, how we love and serve, and the things we say and do will ultimately help others see Jesus in us. Remember what God's Word says:

> You are the light of the world. A town built on a hill cannot be hidden. Neither do people light a lamp and put it under a bowl. Instead they put it on its stand, and

> it gives light to everyone in the house. In the same way, let your light shine before others, that they may see your good deeds and glorify your Father in heaven.
>
> —*Matthew 5:14–16*

Our mission, then, is to draw others out of the darkness we ourselves were once in, by revealing to them the light of Jesus. This is why it became my mission to help others out of anxiety and fear and to write this book! In helping others experience more freedom and less suffering, there is joy. It's healing to shine light into someone else's darkness and witness that darkness flee. It means we're getting to see something good come out of a bad situation, giving purpose to the pain we once experienced. Like a lighthouse whose light can be seen even in the wildest of storms, our purpose is to offer hope and to light the way to salvation in Jesus Christ with our love. Therefore, rather than seeking any special attention or recognition for what we do for others, our only intention should be to become a holy temple for His light to shine through.

At the end of the day, our love will make the greatest difference to the hurting, the broken, and the lost. God's Word confirms this, saying, "And now these three remain: faith, hope and love. But the greatest of these is love" (1 Corinthians 13:13). I'm reminded of what Dr. Martin Luther King Jr. once proclaimed in one of his most famous sermons. He said, "Darkness cannot drive out darkness; only light can do that. Hate cannot drive out hate; only love can do that."

Love has a name, and His name is Jesus. When Jesus came to earth, He came down "as a light, so that no one who believes in [Him] should stay in darkness" (John 12:46). The Light of Jesus could not be overcome by the darkness of this world. Instead, Jesus overcame because of His love for us! Now

His light shines through *you* to lead others back to Him—the only One with the power to rescue and save.

God will open the doors for His light to shine. You will not need to push the doors open on your own. The Lord is faithful. Obey Him wholeheartedly, seek His face continually, stay humble, be sincere in your motives to help others, and His Word promises: "He will make your righteous reward shine like the dawn, your vindication like the noonday sun" (Psalm 37:6). In other words, God's light will not fail to shine through us, helping others find salvation in Jesus Christ.

If it feels like something is holding you back, you can pray and ask God to make His light shine through you. The following prayer is one I wrote especially for this purpose—to commission you as a vessel of God's revelation-light! Will you pray it for yourself now?

> *Heavenly Father, I pray for a fresh anointing of the light of Your Word, the light of Your Presence, and the fire of the Holy Spirit to come upon me now. May it be a glorious light that cannot be contained, but must burst forth into my family, my community, my country, and the whole world.*
>
> *Father, I repent now for any times I have been silent and hid my light from others. Lord, you have placed Your light within me to shine before others that they may turn from their wicked ways and glorify You. Please reveal the power, strength, and beauty of Your light within me in a personal way and show me how You have specifically called me to be a light in this world. Wherever and however You choose to use me, may I shine in a way that others feel as though they have encountered Jesus Christ Himself! I pray for more of You, God, and less of me.*

Father, I pray for more opportunities to be used to break through the darkness in the world with the light of Your love. Please use me as Your hands and feet to feed the hungry, care for the sick, give abundantly, encourage and comfort the downtrodden, loose the chains of oppression, and declare freedom for the captives.

Father, I pray for a breakthrough in every arena of my personal life as well. Shine Your light into every hidden corner or crevice of my heart that may be resistant to Your will. May I put off anything that hinders me from drawing closer to You or loving others. Give me a passion for reading Your Word. And with each verse, chapter, and turning of the page, I ask You to increase the brightness of Your light within me and bring glory to Your Name.

Like a candle, I stand ready to be lit—to receive the fresh anointing You have for me so that I can begin to spread Your light to those You've called me to! And just like a single candle lit at a Christmas Eve service, I believe You can use me to spark a chain reaction, to help fill the world with Your light alongside others who believe in You.

Finally, Father, thank You for sending Jesus, the Light of the World, to save me from my sins. Thank You, Jesus, for loving me and for making a way for me to bring glory to Your Name. I praise and worship You, and it's in Your Holy Name I pray, Amen!

The stories you carry because of what Christ has done in you—especially in freeing you from fear—are a powerful light. In this day and age, when evil abounds and anxiety and fear are commonplace in the hearts of so many, you can make a difference. You can't reach everyone, but you can reach out to those within your sphere of influence—those in your own home, extended family, and friends, as well as those 10 to 12 people that you come into contact with on a regular basis. So don't hold back. Be bold, be brave, and become the light you want to see in the world! Walk in the light as He is in the light, reflect His glory, and let your light shine! Friend, you were made to rise! You were made to shine!

> Arise, shine, for your light has come, and the glory of the LORD rises upon you. See, darkness covers the earth and thick darkness is over the peoples, but the LORD rises upon you and his glory appears over you. Nations will come to your light, and kings to the brightness of your dawn.
>
> —*Isaiah* ***60:1–3***

STEP 10:
LET YOUR LIGHT SHINE BY HELPING OTHERS

STUDY GUIDE

1. What are some ways you can shine your light for God's kingdom?

2. What step of humble obedience could you take this week to demonstrate your faith in the great *I AM*—who promises to be with you?

3. We were chosen to bear witness to the perfect love of God, to point the way to salvation in Jesus Christ. We can't reach everyone, but we can reach out to those within our sphere of influence—those in our own home, extended family, and friends, as well as those 10 to 12 people we come into contact with on a regular basis. Who is God putting on your heart to reach, and what practical ways can you demonstrate God's love starting this month?

4. Reread Romans 12:21. What does this scripture say we are to do when we feel overwhelmed by the evil and darkness in this world? What are some specific ways you can overcome the evil you see and experience with good?

5. Does it feel like something is holding you back from being able to shine God's light and help others effectively? If so, why do you think that is? If it's a lack of opportunity, say a prayer asking God to open a new door for you to love others, and pray again the prayer I wrote for you at the end of this chapter.

PRAYER:

Heavenly Father, Thank You for choosing to reveal Your glory to me through the Spirit of Your Son, Jesus Christ. Thank You for the fact that no matter how difficult my circumstances are or how dark the atmosphere is, I can still choose to shine my light and help others, thereby claiming more territory for Your kingdom. Help me remember You are with me always, allowing me to continue to be a source of light and love to those around me. Reveal to me how to shine in a way that will lead others closer to You. In Jesus' name I pray, Amen.

STEP 11

RENEW YOUR STRENGTH IN THE LORD

But those who hope in the Lord will renew their strength. They will soar on wings like eagles; they will run and not grow weary, they will walk and not be faint.

—Isaiah 40:31

This journey of faith you're on is not for the faint of heart, is it? Obediently aligning ourselves with God's will, doing the work He has called us to do—is not easy. While you may, at times, doubt your strength to press on, the Lord has not once doubted His ability to work in and through you to fulfill His good plans and purposes. You see, our God-given callings will always require a daily, humble dependence on the Lord. On our own, we will never be enough, but with the Lord as our strength, the good work He began in us will be brought to completion (see Philippians 1:6)—not by *our* might, nor by *our* power, but by *His* Spirit. Do not fear this new mountain of a calling the Lord has given you. Do not let it intimidate you. Instead, ask the Lord to renew your strength and learn to fly on the wings of His perfect love for you.

Did you know that monarch butterflies have much to teach us about God's miraculous sustaining power? Amazingly, of all the butterflies God created, the monarch butterfly is the only one that can make birdlike migrations every year, flying some 2,500 miles from north to south for the cold winter months. In an article called "The Monarchs," author Craig Meeker talks about his experience with these marvelous creatures while out on a walk:

> As I looked at the monarchs I thought, "This is impossible. These two pieces of paper flying in the wind. It is impossible for them to reach such a destination so far away." And I came to a conclusion that what makes the Christian move, makes the monarch move and vice versa . . . When you open your heart heavenward in

> faith, God is able to put in there a determined desire to do His will. When you take a step to fulfill that desire, as we open our hearts to Him, He puts power into our hearts to walk with Him.

Like the monarch butterfly, we are nothing more than fragile vessels, easily broken, and yet God chooses to use us to accomplish His will on this earth. He does this through the power of His Holy Spirit! The Bible explains it this way: "But we have this treasure in jars of clay to show that this all-surpassing power is from God and not from us" (2 Corinthians 4:7). We may be hard pressed (see 2 Corinthians 4:8–9), but this is only so Jesus may be glorified all the more through us. It may seem counterintuitive at first, but our weaknesses can actually show off God's strength.

When we realize that our supposed weaknesses and imperfections better position us to be used by God in this world, we won't be so afraid of letting others see who we really are—weaknesses, past failures, and all. Look again at the apostle Paul. Before becoming a believer, Paul violently opposed Christianity. After he began his ministry, Paul had weaknesses that afflicted him daily. The Bible tells us that Paul was given a "thorn" of the flesh (2 Corinthians 12:7). We don't know exactly what that thorn was, but Paul wrote that he pleaded with God three times to remove it. Despite Paul's pleas, God chose to leave that thorn. Like Paul, there may be a thorn God has left in your flesh, an ongoing struggle—but it doesn't have to limit your ability to obey.

Paul had past failures and weaknesses to overcome, and yet God did not allow these things to hinder Paul from spreading the message of the gospel. God used Paul to write most of the New Testament—from inside a prison cell, no less! Paul knew that admitting his problems was the best way to share with others how the power of God had radically transformed him. Thus, God was glorified even more through Paul—not in spite of his weaknesses, but because of them.

When the Lord called me to write this book, I was unaware of all the challenges I would face along the way. Having never written a book before, I had a lot to learn about the craft of writing, where to find agents and publishers who would publish my book, and how to best connect with the people for whom I was writing. Little did I know this was just the beginning. Along with learning all the ins and outs of writing and publishing a book, new health challenges arose. I was diagnosed with irritable bowel syndrome (IBS) after three months of starting to write the manuscript for the book and then fibromyalgia after completing the first draft about two years later.

My circumstances seemed to move from bad to worse the harder I followed after Christ. I remember one morning in particular; I was in my bathroom trying to get ready for work. The pain was so bad I broke down sobbing. On my knees on the bathroom floor, I bowed my head and hung my arms limp, palms up, over the edge of the bathtub, and prayed. Not with words, but with tears in a posture of surrender looking to God to do something to renew my strength. I had nothing left to give, and realistically I didn't see how I could get back up on my feet and go to work that day. That's when my husband walked in. Seeing I needed help, he reached down and wrapped his strong arms around my waist and gently lifted me to my feet. I didn't have the strength to stand on my own, but with the help of my husband, I could rise once again. In that moment, I felt held by my heavenly Father, His everlasting arms underneath me holding me secure (see Deuteronomy 33:27), giving me the strength I needed to finish getting ready and walk out the door.

When I found myself with seemingly nothing left to give, I returned to the Lord for help. Time and again, I asked God to renew my strength to complete the good work He began in me. The strength came, but not right after praying. It came as I stepped out in faith, in obedience to do the work He had given me to do. What I learned was, as I continued to step out in faith and obedience to do the work, God was there to supply me with the physical, mental, emotional, and spiritual strength I needed to keep going. He carved out time for me when I needed more time to write. He brought people into my life to encourage and support me all along the way.

I've also learned there are times when the strength God supplies us with isn't for us to keep going but to let go. Shortly after God renewed my strength to get back up on my feet and head to work on that particularly difficult day, came another day—the day where God called me to surrender my teaching career to Him. I discovered on that day that it required just as much strength to let go as it did to hold on and keep going. As I mentioned in Step 9, it was difficult to walk away from 17 years of teaching, but for health reasons, it became necessary. What I didn't yet understand at the point of letting go was that God had plans to renew my strength for my new role as a stay-at-home wife, mom, and writer.

When God says He will renew our strength, it doesn't mean we are guaranteed physical strength, but God's power working through us to accomplish His will for us on earth. If you notice God is no longer renewing your strength for a particular task or assignment, it could be He wants to display His power through your weakness. It could also be He wants to reposition you to start doing something else.

I don't know what your specific struggles are, but I do know God has chosen you, just as you are, to be a vessel through which salvation in Jesus Christ may be revealed to the world!

God will take the shattered, broken pieces of your life—those areas of weakness that you probably see as most painful or shameful—and create a beautiful mosaic out of them to tell the world the story of His perfect love! You are truly a masterpiece in the making! Just as God spoke to Paul regarding his weaknesses, He also speaks to us, saying, "My grace is sufficient for you, for my power is made perfect in weakness" (2 Corinthians 12:9). God will give you the power to be all He has created and called you to be. Therefore, be joyful and patient in your suffering (see Romans 12:12), knowing it is your weaknesses that make a way for God's grace to enter in. And where His grace is given, His glory will be revealed.

Throughout the Bible, we read about God's grace. In particular, His grace for His chosen people, Israel. Over and over, throughout their history as a nation, we see how God takes their brokenness and redeems it. After 70 years in Babylonian exile, the result of years of continued disobedience and unfaithfulness, God's grace was once again extended to His people. God called a remnant of Israelites to return to Jerusalem, the Holy City, to begin rebuilding it. The high priest Joshua and Zerubbabel, the governor of Judah, led the charge in the reconstruction of the temple.

After their exile, nothing was as it had been—the great temple, the Holy City of Jerusalem, and their relationship with the Lord had been all but destroyed. The Israelites must have wondered how God would help them rebuild the temple given they now lacked the resources and wealth that went into the original build. And would their relationship with the Lord ever be as good as it once had been? Would He bless them as a nation again? Was restoration from such brokenness even possible? *Strong* and *courageous* would not have been words used to describe these people fresh from captivity.

I suspect the Israelites struggled with a *poverty mindset.* A poverty mindset has been described as "a fear that you will never have enough. It holds you back by convincing you that your circumstances will never change for the better" (Wealth of Geeks, "Breaking Free from a Poverty Mindset"). From a Christian perspective, it limits what we believe God is able to do in and through us. It causes us to doubt who we are in Him. It also makes us doubt His provision and love. Unfortunately, we can get so used to experiencing pain and struggle, especially when it has been long and hard, that we begin to accept it as our new normal. This can be a helpful coping strategy when trying to manage a major change, but it can also be harmful. For example, rather than continuing to hold on to hope in the Lord and allowing that hope to motivate us in the work God has called us to do, we allow discouragement to settle in. Just like the Israelites, we look at the magnitude of God's calling and wonder, *How will I ever be able to accomplish all this? Will God really provide all that I need?*

The truth is, what God has called you to *is* impossible for you to accomplish—apart from Him, that is. To receive the strength you need to be who He has called you to be and do the work the Lord has called you to do, you will need to stay in step with the Holy Spirit, pray, and trust God to provide it. I love what Beth Moore says about our callings: "Our God-ordained callings have never been within our grasp. What a man can do on his own, even at his human best, may be helpful to many but it is not his divine calling. What God sets us apart to accomplish has always been well beyond our ability and skill. It takes Jesus to serve Jesus. True callings demand faith and trust and daily dependency."

We demonstrate our trust by stepping out in faith to do the work. That might sound impossible, like the circle of trust in God requires too much from you. You may worry that you are not ready to run with endurance and perseverance (see Hebrews 12:1), but the beauty of this cycle is that you can trust the Lord to be with you to help you. As you trust, He will renew your strength! He confirms this in His Word, saying, "Do not fear, for I am with you; do not be dismayed, for I am your God. I will strengthen you and help you. I will uphold you with my righteous right hand" (Isaiah 41:10). With Christ in you, you are stronger than you know!

When an act of obedience feels risky, we may need the right encouragement to get going, a word from the Lord, reassuring us that He is with us and for us. If we look back at the Israelites, we see that Zerubbabel, the governor of Judah, needed this to fulfill his call to rebuild the temple. While looking down at his own two hands, wondering where he would get the strength he needed to complete the work God called him to, Zerubbabel received encouragement through the prophet Zechariah in the form of a vision from God:

> Then the angel who talked with me returned and woke me up, like someone awakened from sleep. He asked me, "What do you see?" I answered, "I see a solid gold lampstand with a bowl at the top and seven lamps on it, with seven channels to the lamps. Also there are two olive trees by it, one on the right of the bowl and the other on its left." I asked the angel who talked with me, "What are these, my lord?" He answered, "Do you not know what these are?" "No, my lord," I replied. So he said to me, "This is the word of the LORD to Zerubbabel: 'Not by might nor by power, but by my Spirit,' says the LORD Almighty. 'What are you, mighty mountain? Before Zerubbabel you will become level ground.'" . . . Then I asked the angel, "What are these two olive trees on the right and the left of the lampstand?" Again I asked him, "What are these two olive branches be-

side the two gold pipes that pour out golden oil?" He replied, "Do you not know what these are?" "No, my lord," I said. So he said, "These are the two who are anointed to serve the LORD of all the earth."

—Zechariah 4:1–7, 11–14

This passage of Scripture is so rich with symbolism and meaning, providing us with great insight into how the Holy Spirit works in our lives to strengthen us. It's also a little complicated to understand, so I'd like to break it down for you with the wisdom I gained from the research I did. To begin, we read about two olive trees. These represent Zerubbabel and the high priest Joshua. Between the two olive trees is a golden lampstand, which represents Jesus. The golden oil, poured through the golden pipes of the lampstand into the branches of the two olive trees, symbolizes the power of the Holy Spirit infilling Zerubbabel and Joshua with all the strength they would need to do God's work. The Lord explained how Zerubbabel would accomplish the work of rebuilding the temple: "Not by might nor by power, but by my Spirit" (Zechariah 4:6).

The Lord didn't just leave it at that, however. He further revealed to Zerubbabel that both he and Joshua were specifically chosen and anointed for the work they had been called to do. Attaching such significance and purpose to Zerubbabel's life and work would have been hugely motivating and encouraging! If God had chosen and anointed him for the work of rebuilding the temple, then certainly He would be with him to help him accomplish the task. Now, greatly encouraged, Zerubbabel understood that he did not need to depend upon his own strength or power.

God does not want you to fail to obey Him. In the same way the Holy Spirit strengthened Zerubbabel for his role in the work of rebuilding the temple, He will also strengthen you for what He has called you to do! Maybe you've heard it said, *God doesn't call the equipped. He equips the called.* As His Word says, "His divine power has given us everything we need for a godly life through our knowledge of him who called us by his own glory and goodness" (2 Peter 1:3).

Therefore, we must learn to draw our strength from Jesus, our source of life, through the power of His Holy Spirit. Just as the golden oil continuously poured from the golden lampstand into the branches of the two olive trees in the vision, the Holy Spirit will continuously fill you. By faith, you can confidently do all God has called you to do—knowing His strength, His wisdom, His power, His peace, His provision, and His love will never run dry. Can you picture the constant flow of His perfect love being poured into you right now?

We must stay connected to Jesus to receive His power. Jesus is the vine, and we are the branches (see John 15:5). Without the anointing of the Holy Spirit flowing in and through us, we can do nothing of kingdom worth! To stay connected, we need to be in constant communication with Him through prayer and consistent time in His Word. Jesus said, "If you remain in me and my words remain in you, ask whatever you wish, and it will be done for you. This is to my Father's glory, that you bear much fruit, showing yourselves to be my disciples" (John 15:7–8).

If we want God's power and provision for our lives, we must also remain obedient to do the good works God has called us to do. "For we are God's handiwork, created in Christ Jesus *to do good works,* which God prepared in advance for us to do" (Ephesians 2:10, emphasis mine). We are not to go our own way and do whatever we please—God rescues, restores, and releases us to fulfill His plans and purposes. God will *not* bless disobedience. He will not supply you with His divine strength and power to do something that is outside of His will for you. This *new thing* you're embarking on may be the hardest thing you've ever set out to do, but don't let that keep you from rising to the occasion. Shake yourself free from every subtle form of bondage, poverty mindset, and fear. Choose to step out in faith and obedience. Go after what God has called you to do and finish it! The fruit of your labor will absolutely be worth the pain and struggle you will, no doubt, experience. *No pain, no gain*—as the saying goes!

Be careful not to disobey by putting off or delaying the good work the Lord has given you to do either. Delays can easily derail us, causing us to fall out of alignment with God, and delayed obedience *is* disobedience (see Psalm 119:60). According to Haggai, when the remnant of Israelites initially returned to Jerusalem, they did not prioritize rebuilding the temple. They said to one another, "The time has not yet come to rebuild the LORD's house" (Haggai 1:2). Rather than doing what the Lord called them to do, they became consumed with building nice, comfortable homes for themselves and living life on their own terms. "Then the word of the LORD came through the prophet Haggai: 'Is it a time for you yourselves to be living in your paneled houses, while this house remains a ruin?'" (Haggai 1:3–4).

Instead of leading Spirit-empowered, joy-filled, fruitful lives for God, in close relationship with Him, they put God on the back burner. They lost sight of what was most important. As a result, God would no longer bless the work of their hands. To help open their eyes to their sin, God called for a drought on the land, on the people and livestock, and on all their labor (see Haggai 1:11). So even though the Israelites worked hard and planted much, they yielded very little fruit for their labor. His message to them was clear. God was saying, *You are not to go your own way or prioritize anything ahead of Me. If you want My blessing, My power, and My provision for your lives, you will need to seek first My kingdom and do the work I have called you to do. Then you will be blessed, and your work will be fruitful.*

Jesus promised us that the greatest joy and benefit will come when we keep our priorities straight: "Seek first his kingdom and his righteousness, and all these things will be given to you as well" (Matthew 6:33). Don't seek more money or bigger and better things, seek Him. Don't seek better health, seek Him. Don't seek the perfect job, seek Him. Don't even seek His blessing or His deliverance. Seek *God* first!

We should not go our own way and do whatever we please. Rather, we should seek to make the most of every opportunity we receive and live our lives worthy of our high calling in Christ Jesus, who died for us and qualified us to share in His inheritance (see Colossians 1:10–12). This includes making the most of what we do with our physical bodies. "Do you not know that your bodies are temples of the Holy Spirit, who is in you, whom you have received from God? You are not your own; you were bought at a price. Therefore honor God with your bodies" (1 Corinthians 6:19–20). What a privilege it is to house this most precious gift! But stewarding this gift is also quite a responsibility. We must be ready for however God chooses to use us to further His kingdom.

Do you take care to eat well and exercise consistently? Do you maintain your appearance and personal hygiene? What messages do you deliberately (or inadvertently) send to others about your priorities and beliefs? What type of messages are you taking in through your eyes and ears regularly? Think television, movies, music, literature, podcasts, etc. How do you choose to spend your resources of time, money, and energy? Our flesh will want to rebel. There will be other things vying for our attention and affection, but to remain obedient to the

Lord, we must put aside our own fleshly desires and put God first.

Do not confuse obedience to God with a life of ease. If you are a follower of Jesus, you will almost certainly face opposition to the work the Lord has called you to. This doesn't mean you have gotten off track with Him or are doing something wrong. Some people believe—falsely—that if you stay in line and do everything right, only good things will happen to you. This is simply not the case. Oftentimes, the stronger your faith, the more likely you are to become a target for the enemy, facing trials and persecution. I believe God allows this to give us an opportunity to faithfully walk through it with Him and bring glory to His name.

In their efforts to rebuild the temple, the Israelites faced severe opposition from their enemies, the surrounding peoples. These people set out to discourage them and to make them afraid to go on building. They did not want to see Israel rise in strength and power. When mere discouragement didn't work, they decided to intensify their efforts. They fought dirty. At one point, the opposition against Israel became so fierce the temple reconstruction had to come to a complete stop. Weak and weary, the Israelites became discouraged.

It's easy to get discouraged, isn't it? When we observe what seems like such minimal progress in the work God has called us to, it's hard to be patient, persevere, and trust in God's sovereign plans. When we lose our momentum, it's easy to get distracted and forget why we ever started the work in the first place. The best thing we can do is to recalibrate ourselves with our "why." Our *why* is our reason for starting, and it's what keeps us moving toward our end goal. It's what helps us maintain self-control and discipline all along the way. Our *why* helps us persevere when faced with opposition. You may have many different reasons why you do what you do, and that is okay. However, as believers, we ultimately do everything we do for the Lord. This makes Jesus, our *why*. Jesus is the ultimate prize!

> Do you not know that in a race all the runners run, but only one gets the prize? Run in such a way as to get the prize. Everyone who competes in the games goes into strict training. They do it to get a crown that will not last, but we do it to get a crown that will last forever. Therefore I do not run like someone running aimlessly; I do not fight like a boxer beating the air. No, I strike a blow to my body and make it my slave so that after I have preached to others, I myself will not be disqualified for the prize.
>
> —*1 Corinthians 9:24–27*

It takes perseverance to run a good race. Many start out strong, but few continue to follow and obey Jesus all the way to the finish line. To which the Lord says, "You were running a good race. Who cut in on you to keep you from obeying the truth?" (Galatians 5:7). The thing is, if something or someone is keeping you from following the Lord, that should raise a red flag in your heart. Keep your eyes on the prize! Remember your *why*! Finish your race!

Why do our best-laid plans so often fail? The problem is we can work hard and strive to achieve, but if we are relying on our own strength, we'll soon discover—along with millions of other people around the world—we've entered into the wrong race: the "rat race." That is, the race the world has determined we must run if we want to do or be anything of significance. In the *rat race,* we become so exhausted from mindlessly trying to keep up with all the other "rats" that we burn out. This is purposeless living. The Lord also calls this type of behavior into question, saying, "Are you so foolish? After beginning by means of the Spirit, are you now trying to finish by means of the flesh?" (Galatians 3:3).

We may think that by pushing harder, we will please God with the "good job" we are doing for Him, but all this does is highlight our own arrogance and pride. The Bible makes it clear, "Unless the LORD builds the house, the builders labor in vain" (Psalm 127:1). Striving to do more than what God asks will not lead to greater productivity, it will lead to anxiety. This sort of striving is rooted in fear, not faith. The bottom line: unless we rely on the Holy Spirit to empower us for God's good works, we should not expect to accomplish anything of eternal value.

Remember Zechariah 4 and the encouragement the Lord provided Zerubbabel in his calling to rebuild the temple? Verses 8–9 say, "Then the word of the LORD came to me: 'The hands of Zerubbabel have laid the foundation of this temple; his hands will also complete it'" (Zechariah 4:8–9). In other words, God promised that He would bring to completion the good work He began in Zerubbabel. It was a mountain of a task, but the Lord reassured him that the mountain would become level ground before Zerubbabel.

How often are we just like Zerubbabel? Looking down at our own two hands, doubting we have what it takes to finish our race? When things felt too heavy, I used to pray that God would take away my weariness and move the mountains out of my way. However, whenever I prayed this prayer, I rarely got much relief.

There are times God chooses to leave the mountains in our way. Not to oppress us, but to help us grow in our faith. God wants to demonstrate to us His power to overcome. He wants us to finish strong! Just as the Lord called Zerubbabel to be a mountain mover, He also calls us to move mountains. Not in our own strength or power, of course, but in the strength and power that only He can provide. God's Word says, "Truly I tell you, if you have faith as small as a mustard seed, you can say to this mountain, 'Move from here to there,' and it will move. Nothing will be impossible for you" (Matthew 17:20). God can move the mountains for you, but He wants you to boldly and confidently assert your authority as an heir to the kingdom of God and declare by faith, "Mountain, by the power of Jesus Christ in me, you must move!"

Wherever you are right now, whatever step you're on in your journey toward living perfectly loved, I believe the Lord wants to say to you:

> *Do not despise small beginnings. Remember, with faith the size of a mustard seed, you can move mountains. I've got a mountain for you to move. Not all at once, but one step at a time, hand in hand with Me. With one breath from My Spirit, I will refresh your soul. I will renew your strength. You will know just what to do when My Holy Spirit comes upon you. Stay connected to Me, the one true Vine, and I will empower you to accomplish My will on the earth. You have been chosen for such a time as this, for a specific purpose. There is a good reason for you to be hope-filled. I am with you. I have all you need. I AM all you need.*

Can you relate to the difficulties the Israelites faced in their plight to remain faithful to the Lord and to rebuild the temple? By grace, through faith in Jesus Christ, the Holy Spirit breathes His life into us—giving us strength and power to do His will. This strength is not only enough to help us keep putting one foot in front of the other—it is enough to raise the dead, heal the sick, and cast out demons. If you are a believer, His power is alive in you!

The Israelites did eventually complete the temple. Their God-given task was accomplished with the Lord as their strength. But it was never about the completion of a task; rather, God wanted to reconcile His relationship with His people. The temple was merely the means through which God could draw His people closer to Himself. The process of rebuilding helped the Israelites recognize their need for God. It caused them to depend on Him daily for strength. It rekindled their desire for a closer relationship with Him. It renewed their hope and faith. And as it turned out, the glory of the second temple outshone the first!

Isn't that just like what God does with us? He allows our brokenness, our weaknesses, our failures, and our limitations to be the catalyst for our dependence on Him. He uses the work we do for Him as an opportunity to draw us closer. Ultimately, we will realize it's never about the work we are doing for the Lord, but about who we are becoming in relationship with Him.

The Bible tells us in Philippians 1:6, "He who began a good work in you will carry it on to completion until the day of Christ Jesus." God has always intended for you to be filled to the measure with His goodness, confident in His presence, full of faith and joy, heart at rest, and perfected in His love! There is hard work yet to be done, but you can do hard things! The Lord is with you! Though we can easily lose hope and get discouraged when life's struggles seem too much to bear, God renews our hope and our strength. We are never alone.

I wrote the following prose to help you remember that God is with you and He is for you. Use it when you're beginning to despair or lose hope to awaken the courage the Lord has planted deep within you. May it revive your spirit and encourage you to persevere and finish your race.

Awake, my soul, awake! Arise! The LORD your God is with you! Though you stumble, you will not fall. Remember, the LORD has made a way for you, alighting the path before you. Surely, you will rise in triumph over your enemies. Your foes will be no more. Rise up now, on the wings of His perfect love for you! Delight yourself in Him, and He will give you the desires of your heart. Your life is not over yet, child. There is still work here to be done. Begin again to sing His praises! It's time to begin again! Is the joy of the LORD *not your strength? Awake, my soul, awake! Arise!*

Don't give up! Keep going! It's time to dig deep within yourself! Strength doesn't come from doing what you think you can do. It comes from stepping out in faith and obedience to what God has called you to do—believing His strength will rise up to meet you. Therefore, "be strong and courageous, and do the work. Do not be afraid or discouraged, for the LORD God, my God, is with you. He will not fail you or forsake you until all the work for the service of the temple of the LORD is finished" (1 Chronicles 28:20).

> Surely God is my salvation; I will trust and not be afraid. The LORD, the LORD himself, is my strength and my song; he has become my salvation.
>
> ***—ISAIAH 12:2***

STEP 11:
RENEW YOUR STRENGTH IN THE LORD

STUDY GUIDE

1. In what area(s) of your life have you tried to rely on your own strength?

2. Is there something you sense God calling you to do, but you don't think you have the strength to do it? Reread Zechariah 4:6. What would you do if you knew you could not fail?

3. Reread Matthew 17:20. Is there a mountain in your way that God has not yet moved for you? What purpose might God have for this mountain?

4. Reread John 15:5. Why is it important we stay connected to "the Vine"?

5. How does the Holy Spirit help us in our weakness?

6. Our faith is made complete by what we do. Name at least one way you can put your faith into action this week.

PRAYER:

Heavenly Father, Thank You for helping me do the work You've called me to do! I confess there are days when I struggle, fail, and feel intimidated by the mountains before me. I question whether I am enough. But then You remind me of who I am: I am a child of God. I believe I am chosen, and I can move mountains! Thank You for Your Holy Spirit's presence, which strengthens me daily and encourages me to never give up. Father, help me feel the power of Your Holy Spirit flowing through me. May I never rely upon my strength but on Your strength alone to empower me to follow and obey You. In Jesus' name I pray, Amen.

STEP 12

LOVE FEARLESSLY

And so we know and rely on the love God has for us. God is love. Whoever lives in love lives in God, and God in them.

—1 John 4:16

"There is no fear in love. But perfect love drives out fear . . ." (1 John 4:18). This verse of Scripture has been the theme I've weaved into each step of our journey to living perfectly loved. I pray it has served as a reminder that you are safe in the perfect love of God, forever secure in His grip. Therefore, you need not *ever* fear because God is love, and you are found in Him! Having been rescued from your bondage to fear, restored in your relationship with Christ, and released to shine the light of Jesus into this dark world, you can finally embrace the freedom and fullness of life found in Christ alone. You can live perfectly loved—remembering God is with you and His perfect love will always be enough—and begin to love others fearlessly. This is what life's all about. This is your destiny!

When I think about what it means to love fearlessly, I think of the patron saint of Ireland, St. Patrick. Many people celebrate St. Patrick's life and work as a missionary and priest each year on March 17th. He is known as the "Apostle of Ireland" for being among the first to successfully spread the gospel message throughout Ireland in the fifth century, until which time it had been a mostly pagan nation.

What many people do not know is that St. Patrick wasn't even Irish! According to "The Real St. Patrick," an article written by Ted Olsen for Christianity Today, "Patrick was 16 years old in about the year 405, when he was captured in a raid and became a slave in what was still radically pagan Ireland." He was kidnapped from his home in what's now Dumbarton, Scotland, and forced to work as a herdsman in Ireland. It was during this time of bondage to his captors that St. Patrick's relationship with the Lord was cultivated and ultimately matured. God used difficult circumstances to draw St. Patrick closer to Him. After six long years of bondage spent mostly in prayer, St. Patrick escaped his captors and finally returned home to his parents. As the story goes, though, the Lord called St. Patrick to return to Ireland some years later, likely when he was in his mid-forties, to share the gospel of Jesus Christ with the very same people who had abducted and enslaved him!

Can you imagine? God called St. Patrick to love his enemies in a way that is hard for most of us to fathom. As a child, I was sensitive, quiet, and shy but also quick to become defensive if I felt misunderstood or hurt emotionally. My Irish-Catholic grandfather used to say to me, "Stay on the offense, not the defense!" I believe this was his way of encouraging me not to get angry and defensive with people who accuse me or fail to love me the way I wish they would, but to remain calm and secure with who and whose I am instead. It was also his way of telling me not to be timid and afraid in my approach with people, but rather bold and fearless. His words remind me of the way St. Patrick chose to love the people of Ireland.

While St. Patrick could have easily taken a self-protective, defensive stance and refused to return to Ireland for fear of what his former heathen captors might do to him, he didn't. Instead, he took an offensive approach. Allowing Jesus' love for the unsaved people of Ireland to fill his heart, St. Patrick was emboldened to step out in faith and boldly proclaim the name of Jesus to the broken, the hurting, and the lost. Selflessly, he loved the people of Ireland more than he loved his own life—and praise God he did! As a result of St. Patrick's decision to love fearlessly, a nation of people was saved for eternity! Jesus has called each of us to love others in this way.

I believe God wants us to understand that no matter how dark or painful our circumstances may be or how intense the opposition to our faith, we always have a choice as to how we will respond: in fear or in love. When we react in fear, we tend to respond defensively, putting up walls of self-protection around us. This keeps us from being able to continue loving those around us, as well as receiving love from others. On the other hand, when we respond in love courageously and compassionately, we will be empowered to release responsibility for our protection to God, trusting Him to come to our defense (see Isaiah 52:12). We will come to rely on God's perfect love to fill us rather than the imperfect love of other people. This will free us to focus on loving those whom God has called us to love joyfully and wholeheartedly.

Personally, I have learned in my struggle with the fear of rejection and abandonment that I can be tempted to withhold my love from people. Having been deeply hurt by people who have neglected to love me, rejected me, or abandoned me, it can feel safer to put up walls of self-protection around my heart rather than risk vulnerability, opening myself up to further pain. I may say to myself, *Because they don't fill my cup, I will no longer fill theirs*, and continue the cycle of rejection and abandonment. However, this wouldn't be the right response because as painful as it sometimes is to love them, I know these are people in my life whom God has called me to love fearlessly.

Rather than fear their rejection and abandonment, I choose to remember that Jesus took up the pain of my being rejected and abandoned and laid it upon Himself so I would never have to carry the weight of that pain ever again. I can remember His unfailing love and acceptance, and instead of looking to other people to fill my cup and make me feel whole, I can let go of the unholy expectations I've had of others and look to God, whose perfect love will always be enough to meet my every need. This will allow me the freedom to continue to love without fear. (Note: This doesn't include abusive people from whom you need to keep a safe distance or those with a pattern of hurtful or harmful behavior with whom you establish boundaries to protect your physical, financial, emotional, and spiritual health. You may choose to love these individuals from a distance by praying for them, for example, or in other ways that don't compromise your health and safety, depending on your relationship with them.)

I believe this is the offensive position my grandfather encouraged me to take. It seems both St. Patrick and my grandfather understood what I'm still learning to live out: we can be joy-filled and free in choosing to love fearlessly, knowing we are completely covered and protected by God's perfect love! Yes, to love fearlessly comes with risk, but it's a risk worth taking when God is with you, guiding you in it.

For another example of what it looks like to love fearlessly, let's look at how Peter and John, two of Jesus' disciples, responded in Acts 4 when they were told by the Sanhedrin they would have to stop teaching about Jesus or be severely punished. "But Peter and John replied, 'Which is right in God's eyes: to listen to you, or to him? You be the judges! As for us, we cannot help speaking about what we have seen and heard'" (Acts 4:19–20).

This was an extremely courageous response! The Sanhedrin was composed of the most powerful Jewish leaders in all Israel, with the authority to rule like judges in the supreme court. How did Peter and John act so fearlessly when facing such severe persecution for their faith? The Bible tells us the people "realized that they were unschooled, ordinary men" (Acts 4:13). In other words, there was nothing extraordinary about them to give them a leg up against the rulers of their faith. But Acts 4:18 reveals the answer: because Peter was "filled with the Holy Spirit," he was able to speak with such great courage when threatened by the Sanhedrin. What a great testimony to God's perfect love driving out fear.

You may recall hearing other Bible stories involving Peter—such as before Jesus' death and resurrection and at Pentecost—when Peter wasn't always so bold and courageous. In John 18, when Jesus was arrested by Roman soldiers and taken away to be crucified, not one of His disciples stood by Him. They all ran away afraid, including Peter. Not only had Peter run, but just as Jesus predicted Peter would, he denied ever having known Jesus, disowning Him—not once, not twice, but *three times*.

As a result, Peter became consumed with guilt and shame. When Jesus was no longer physically present to show him what to do, Peter returns to the only thing he knew how to do: fishing. (And even that didn't go well.) In John 21, we read that Peter and a few of the other disciples went out fishing one night. But after working all night, the disciples came up empty-handed.

Then seemingly out of nowhere, they heard a familiar voice calling out to them about a hundred yards from shore. It was Jesus, although they did not yet recognize Him. Jesus asked, "Friends, haven't you any fish?" (John 21:5). Jesus told them to try letting down their nets again, but this time on the right side of the boat. They did this and miraculously ended up with so many fish they couldn't haul them all in. But it wasn't until John said to Peter, "It is the Lord!" (John 21:7), that Peter looked up and realized it was Jesus. At once, Peter jumped out of the boat and ran to shore to meet Him.

As excited as Peter was to see Jesus, he was still carrying around the guilt and shame of having disowned Jesus. Jesus knew this, of course. So after they finished eating the fish and bread Jesus had prepared for them, Jesus approached Peter and said to him:

> "Simon son of John, do you truly love me more than these?" "Yes, Lord," he said, "you know that I love you." Jesus said, "Feed my lambs." Again Jesus said, "Simon son of John, do you love me?" He answered, "Yes, Lord, you know that I love you." Jesus said, "Take care of my sheep." The third time he said to him, "Simon son of John, do you love me?" Peter was hurt because Jesus asked him the third time, "Do you love me?" He said, "Lord, you know all things; you know that I love you." Jesus said, "Feed my sheep."
>
> —***John 21:15–17***

Although Peter had failed to love fearlessly in what was arguably the darkest hour of human history, Jesus had not stopped loving Peter. Rather than shame Peter for his failures, He forgave him and offered Peter another crack at being a faithful follower. Jesus used the miracle of the huge catch of fish to remind Peter, as well as the other disciples with him, that if they would choose to follow Him, to seek first His kingdom, and to love fearlessly, they would be fruitful in their work. However, should they choose to shrink back in fear and return to their old ways of living, they would surely continue to come up empty-handed with nothing of eternal value to show for their efforts.

After asking Peter three times whether he loved Him, Jesus revealed to Peter the kind of death he would experience in choosing to be His disciple. Then Jesus said to him, "Follow me!" (John 21:19). It was decision time. Peter could choose to love fearlessly and to follow Jesus wholeheartedly, knowing that one day this would result in martyrdom, or he could choose to walk away from the greatest love he'd ever known and live an empty, shallow life. Jesus didn't sugarcoat the realities of what this choice would mean for Peter. He laid it all out there in the open for him. Peter, of course, recommitted to following Jesus and eventually willingly laid down his life for the cause of Christ.

Likewise, there will come a point when you must make a decision about your commitment level to Christ. You must ask yourself, like Peter, *Am I willing to lay down my life for Jesus? Am I all in?* John 12:25 says, "Anyone who loves their life will lose it, while anyone who hates their life in this world will keep it for eternal life." If we continue to live defensively, seeking self-protection at all costs, I believe this verse is saying we will miss out on the fullness of life God has made available to us now (see John 6:63), along with "the crown of life that the Lord has promised to those who love him" (James 1:12).

Jesus asks us, *Do you love me? Do you truly love me?* To love Jesus is to follow Him—even unto death, should it ever come to that. Jesus warns:

> But before all this, they will seize you and persecute you. They will hand you over to synagogues and put you in prison, and you will be brought before kings and governors, and all on account of my name. And so you will bear testimony to me. But make up your mind not to worry beforehand how you will defend yourselves. For I will give you words and wisdom that none of your adversaries will be able to resist or contradict. You will be betrayed even by parents, brothers and sisters, relatives and friends, and they will put some of you to death. Everyone will hate you because of me. But not a hair of your head will perish. Stand firm, and you will win life.
>
> ***—Luke 21:12–19***

You will win life? I love this! Who doesn't like to win, am I right? Again, though, we must stand firm until the end. While it's hard to face the prospect of becoming a martyr for Christ, this is a reality we must consider and even accept as a real possibility when we decide to follow Jesus. Your enemy, the devil, will try to make you too afraid to continue on, but don't let this stop you! Instead, choose to keep loving fearlessly in unity with other believers in the body of Christ, like Peter, John, and the other disciples, and make Jesus known to the world. Yes, fear may still be present, but in Christ we will overcome it.

Jesus said to His disciples, "Therefore go and make disciples of all nations, baptizing them in the name of the Father and of the Son and of the Holy Spirit, and teaching them to obey everything I have commanded you. And surely I am with you always, to the very end of the age" (Matthew 28:19–20).

This commissioning of Jesus' original disciples, known widely as the Great Commission, also applies to us, Jesus' disciples today. Notice that Jesus did not say, *Stay safe inside your nice, comfortable homes and keep to yourselves.* Or *Only love those who will love you back.* No: He said, *Go and make disciples of all nations!* Love all people by showing them the way to salvation in Jesus Christ and testifying to all He has done.

Knowing we could never do this in our own power, Jesus gifted us with His Holy Spirit to lead and guide us. Jesus said, "But you will receive power when the Holy Spirit comes on you; and you will be my witnesses in Jerusalem, and in all Judea and Samaria, and to the ends of the earth" (Acts 1:8). This is how Jesus' disciple Peter, who was once cowardly and afraid, became the apostle Peter who courageously declared His faith in Jesus Christ before the Sanhedrin. You can be courageous too. As a believer in Jesus Christ, the same Spirit that was alive in Peter is very much alive in you. One practical way to cling to the truth of God's perfect love and to renew your spirit in preparation for loving others fearlessly is to begin each day with prayer and meditation. The following prayer, commonly attributed to St. Patrick, is an abbreviated version of the

"Breastplate of St. Patrick," a prayer used within the Catholic tradition. You can use it to help you visualize that Jesus is with you always to protect you, and there is absolutely nothing to fear:

> I arise today, through
> God's strength to pilot me,
> God's might to uphold me,
> God's wisdom to guide me,
> God's eye to look before me,
> God's ear to hear me,
> God's word to speak for me,
> God's hand to guard me,
> God's shield to protect me,
> God's host to save me . . .
>
> Christ with me,
> Christ before me,
> Christ behind me,
> Christ in me,
> Christ beneath me,
> Christ above me,
> Christ on my right,
> Christ on my left,
> Christ when I lie down,
> Christ when I sit down,
> Christ when I arise,
> Christ in the heart of every man who thinks of me,
> Christ in the mouth of everyone who speaks of me,
> Christ in every eye that sees me,
> Christ in every ear that hears me.
>
> —*Anonymous*

Remember, 1 John 4:18 told us that the prescription for fear is God's perfect love. It says, "There is no fear in love. But perfect love drives out fear, because fear has to do with punishment. The one who fears is not made perfect in love." Once fear has been driven out of our lives and God's love has been *made perfect* in us, 1 John 4:19 tells us that we are to "love because he first loved us."

We are to bear witness to the perfect love of Jesus in the love we show others. Healed and whole, we can allow the love that fills us to flow out and into the hearts of those who desperately need to know God loves them! Jesus says this in John 13:34–35: "A new command I give you: Love one another. As I have loved you, so you must love one another. By this everyone will know that you are my disciples, if you love one another."

In theory, this should be relatively simple. Simple doesn't always mean easy, though, does it? The Bible says, "Love is patient, love is kind. It does not envy, it does not boast, it is not proud. It does not dishonor others, it is not self-seeking, it is not easily angered, it keeps no record of wrongs. Love does not delight in evil but rejoices with the truth. It always protects, always trusts, always hopes, always perseveres. Love never fails" (1 Corinthians 13:4–8).

That's a tall order! Loving others the way God has called us to love isn't easy. If only we could keep it simple and not try to complicate it. Yet so often we overthink it. We shrink back from inviting coworkers to church because we believe they will probably say no. We think about telling a friend our testimony but don't because they might think we're weird and no longer want to be friends with us. We hesitate to share a Bible verse on social media because we don't want anyone to call us a Bible-thumping Christian, lump us in with people who spew hatred, get called intolerant and backward . . . what if I get canceled? We withhold our love because we fear the world more than we fear God. We want people to like us. We don't want to face the potential backlash for choosing to obey God, so we make excuses for why we can't do what God calls us to do. We may think we are being discerning and wise in selectively waiting for just the right opportunity to come along to share the good news of Jesus Christ—but are we? Could there be a fine line between fear and faithfulness, such that withholding our love means we are actually choosing to act in fear?

God takes loving others very seriously. The Bible says in 1 Corinthians 13:1–3 that we can be blessed with spiritual gifts, strive to serve others, and have faith enough to move mountains—but if we do it all without love, we've gained nothing. In fact, we *are* nothing (see 1 Corinthians 1:2). In other words, all my effort to try and please God with the good things I'm doing is worthless if I do not also love. I don't know about you, but for me, as someone who can focus too much on task completion rather than being present with people, these words are very convicting.

While we will never be able to love others perfectly, the way only God can, this cannot be an excuse for holding back any longer. Instead, we must learn to receive the perfect love that God has always had for us and begin to point people to Jesus by allowing His perfect love to flow through us. This is how we do our part to fulfill the Great Commission—to *go and make disciples of all nations!*

Unfortunately, not everyone you love fearlessly will be open to receiving your love. Not every person you feel led to share the gospel with will wholeheartedly respond to the message and choose salvation. There will be times when the darkness will feel overpowering, when people will hate you for loving them. But don't give up! "On the contrary: 'If your enemy is hungry, feed him; if he is thirsty, give him something to drink. In doing this, you will heap burning coals on his head.' Do not be overcome by evil, but overcome evil with good"

(Romans 12:20–21). Regardless of how people respond, you have been called to act in love.

Does this mean we are like sheep being led to the slaughter? Are we putting ourselves out there only to get crushed? The Bible says:

> No, in all these things we are more than conquerors through him who loved us. For I am convinced that neither death nor life, neither angels nor demons, neither the present nor the future, nor any powers, neither height nor depth, nor anything else in all creation, will be able to separate us from the love of God that is in Christ Jesus our Lord.
>
> ***—Romans 8:37–39***

Confident, then, that nothing will ever be able to separate you from God's perfect love, ask yourself this: *Will I let the fear of someone be greater than my love for them—greater than God's love for me?*

In the book *One Thousand Gifts*, author Ann Voskamp defines fear. She writes as though God were speaking directly to us:

> All fear is the notion that God's love ends. Do you think I end, that My bread warehouses are limited, that I will not be enough? But I am infinite, child. What can end in Me? Can life end in Me? Can happiness? Or peace? Or anything you need? I am the Bread of Life and My bread for you will never end. Fear thinks God is finite and fear believes that there is not going to be enough . . .

Since we now know that God's love is perfect and that we need not fear that His love for us will ever end, let us cling to this truth and begin to step out and love others without fear—knowing that the love of Christ will never fail to protect, provide, and fill us. We can count on the perfect love of Jesus. His love is all we need. It will always be enough.

Jesus knew His disciples would face severe persecution for following Him and struggle to love fearlessly (and that we would too). It's for this reason Jesus prayed for them (and us) in the Garden of Gethsemane before going to the cross. He prayed: "I have given them your word and the world has hated them, for they are not of the world any more than I am of the world. My prayer is not that you take them out of the world but that you protect them from the evil one" (John 17:14–15). Jesus also told His disciples, "If the world hates you, keep in mind that it hated me first" (John 15:18).

As disciples of Jesus Christ today, we can expect to join in His suffering. Philippians 1:29 further confirms this, saying, "For it has been granted to you on behalf of Christ not only to believe in him, but also to suffer for him." Jesus' prayer was not that the Father would keep us from experiencing pain and suffering in this world, but rather that the Father would protect us from the devil who tries to prevent us from continuing to love God and love others. No, Jesus didn't want His disciples, or us, to shrink back in fear, but rather to go confidently into all the world and preach the gospel. Jesus said to His disciples, "The harvest is plentiful but the workers are few" (Matthew 9:37). I believe the servant of the Lord responds in her heart, *Pick me, Lord, send me!*

In the Garden of Gethsemane, Jesus also prayed for all believers—including you and me (see John 17:20–26). Jesus prayed that we would live loved, in perfect unity with Him and the Father through the indwelling of the Holy Spirit. He also prayed we would live in perfect unity with other believers—as one body with Christ as the head. He prayed for unity—us in Him and Him in us—because the believer who knows they are perfectly loved will love fearlessly. They will live their lives not for themselves, but in perfect unity with fellow believers in the body of Christ for the cause of Christ. This way the whole world will see and know that Jesus truly came down from the Father to save people from their sins and to restore what was lost—unity and fellowship with God who loves them. Jesus prayed:

> Father, I want those you have given me to be with me where I am, and to see my glory, the glory you have given me because you loved me before the creation of the world. Righteous Father, though the world does not know you, I know you, and they know that you have sent me. I have made you known to them, and will continue to make you known in order that the love you have for me may be in them and that I myself may be in them.
>
> —*John 17:24–26*

When Jesus prayed for all believers in the Garden of Gethsemane, what touches my heart most deeply is that He was praying for His future bride! We, the church, the whole body of believers, are the beloved bride of Christ. We are betrothed to Jesus! In His prayer, we can sense the passion and intensity with which Jesus prayed for all those who would one day come to know Him as their Lord and Savior.

Like a bride and groom eagerly await their wedding day, our bridegroom Jesus has been praying for the day when we will finally be united with Him for all eternity! He is filled with love for His bride. She is the one He adores. He is calling to her, passionately pursuing a relationship with her. He wants all of her and will stop at nothing to get her. He wants to be one with her. He wants her to be with Him where He is. His heart longs for her! Likewise, the bride of Christ is enamored with her husband. Her King sits enthroned, and she longs for the day when she will finally see Him face-to-face—when He will wipe away every tear from her eyes, and she will gaze deeply into His.

Have you ever watched the groom's face as he watches his bride walk down the aisle toward him on their wedding day? The look on his face says it all. It speaks of his love for his bride, his undying devotion, and the anticipation he feels for the moment when she will finally be his. He is overwhelmed by her beauty. He sees her, dressed in white, made ready for the moment the two of them will finally become one flesh. In the same way, Jesus looks lovingly on His bride and beckons her. "Come to me!" Jesus calls to us. And we respond, "Come, Lord Jesus!" The steps to the altar will take a lifetime, but when we finally see Jesus face-to-face, we will be united for all eternity. It will be a feeling of great joy and even ecstasy!

Jesus is closely watching us as we put one foot in front of the other, seeing to it that we continue growing and maturing in our faith. He watches as we love others with the love He has given us. He sees our acts of kindness, the way we bless, encourage, and pray for others. He hears us share the message of His love, the gospel, with those who will also someday be joined together with Him in the body of Christ. With each step, we countdown the days until Christ, our Bridegroom, returns for us, and the wedding proceedings will commence! No one but the Father knows when that day will be. Oh, but what a day it will be.

Yes, Jesus' love for His bride strongly emanated through His prayer in the garden, but why did He make such a point to pray also for unity among believers? Why was it so important to Jesus that He let it be His final plea to the Father—His last will and testament—before going to the cross? It's because unity among believers produces the greatest witness! Jesus said, "For where two or three gather in my name, there am

I with them" (Matthew 18:20). God desires for us to be in unity with other believers because that is where He will be, and thus, that is how the world will come to know Him and be reconciled to Him.

Did you know that Aaron, the first high priest to the Israelites, was generously anointed before beginning his ministry? Oil was poured over his head. It ran down his beard and over his garments. With this oil, sometimes referred to as the "oil of unity," he was given the spiritual power and authority to minister to God's people, thereby bringing unity between God and man. God's Word says, "How good and pleasant it is when God's people live together in unity! It is like precious oil poured on the head, running down on the beard, running down on Aaron's beard, down on the collar of his robe" (Psalm 133:1–2).

Like Aaron, you too have been anointed by the Holy Spirit with the oil of unity for this special purpose: to "fearlessly make known the mystery of the gospel" (Ephesians 6:19). You are not alone in this purpose; you are working in unity with all members of the body of Christ to reconcile all things to Christ! This is also known as the ministry of reconciliation, and because we cannot reconcile all things to Christ on our own, we must be connected to the church. "For just as each of us has one body with many members, and these members do not all have the same function, so in Christ we, though many, form one body, and each member belongs to all the others" (Romans 12:4–5).

Having community with others in the body of believers is so important. The greatest good is produced when all parts of the body of Christ are working together. As one body, with Christ as the head (see Ephesians 1:22–23), we were called to peace and unity with one another. God's Word confirms this:

> Therefore, as God's chosen people, holy and dearly loved, clothe yourselves with compassion, kindness, humility, gentleness and patience. Bear with each other and forgive one another if any of you has a grievance against someone. Forgive as the Lord forgave you. And over all these virtues put on love, which binds them all together in perfect unity. Let the peace of Christ rule in your hearts, since as members of one body you were called to peace. And be thankful. Let the message of Christ dwell among you richly as you teach and admonish one another with all wisdom through psalms, hymns, and songs from the Spirit, singing to God with gratitude in your hearts. And whatever you do, whether in word or deed, do it all in the name of the Lord Jesus, giving thanks to God the Father through him.
>
> —*Colossians 3:12–17*

We all have different gifts, and yet we are called to work together for the cause of Christ. If one believer is gifted with an ability to teach, while another is gifted with an ability to heal, should we value one's gifting over the other? No, of course not. Each believer's gifting is of great value to the kingdom of God.

Let us rejoice with other believers when their work or ministry is successful rather than allowing jealousy or pride to divide us. We are not in competition against other believers; we are all on the same team, working for God's kingdom. Because we are part of the same team, we can come alongside believers who are struggling to offer support and encouragement. If one part of the body suffers, the whole body suffers. We need to be cheering each other on!

In the garden, Jesus ends His prayer promising that He would continue to make Himself known to us so that we will increase in the knowledge of God's love for us. In John

15:9, Jesus said, "As the Father has loved me, so have I loved you. Now remain in my love." As we continue to grow in our knowledge and understanding of God's perfect love for us by the power of the Holy Spirit, we will also continue to grow in our wisdom of how to love others. God's Word explains it this way:

> Instead, speaking the truth in love, we will grow to become in every respect the mature body of him who is the head, that is, Christ. From him the whole body, joined and held together by every supporting ligament, grows and builds itself up in love, as each part does its work.
>
> —***Ephesians 4:15–16***

It's not always easy following Jesus. There are hardships and daily sacrifices in choosing to love God and love others. In this life, we will face trials, rejection, abandonment, and persecution. People will betray us. At times it will take every ounce of strength we have to keep going and believing. We may have to endure more pain and suffering than we ever imagined possible for a night, but remember, joy comes in the morning! Jesus said, "In this world you will have trouble. But take heart! I have overcome the world" (John 16:33). The road may seem long at times, but knowing Jesus has us exactly where He wants us on the road to living perfectly loved should give us confidence that He will fulfill His purpose in us. Heaven is not so far away. The complete restoration that is to come when Jesus returns gives us hope of the fulfillment of all God's promises.

Although we are not *of* this world (see John 17:16), we are *in* this world for a purpose—to share the good news of Jesus Christ. Our lives are not our own. We were bought at a price. Sometimes we want to fight God on this. We want to live life on our own terms. We pray that God would make life easier or that He would take us out of whatever situation we are in—or better yet, out of this world altogether and wrap us in His loving arms. We don't always want to do what God is calling us to do for fear of what might happen to us. We groan with longing for His perfection, the fulfillment of His promises, and His kingdom come. All the while, God reminds us that His grace is sufficient, His love is enough, and we have nothing to fear.

What it all boils down to is this: Until we know and believe we are perfectly loved by God and learn to rely on His perfect love, we cannot truly, wholeheartedly, or joyfully love others. When we're secure in God's perfect love, we will discover we are free to love without fear. As we then choose to step out in faith and love fearlessly, God's love is made perfect in us (see 1 John 4:12). This is how we begin living perfectly loved!

And this is what it means to live perfectly loved: Not that everything in your life is now "perfect" or that you are no longer experiencing pain, heartache, disappointment, stress, or anxiety of any kind. However, in spite of your struggles—past, present, and future—you can now say with confidence that the love of Jesus has so transformed your heart and mind that it is now spilling out into every area of your life. Determined not to hide your light anymore, you allow God's love to shine through you and to strive each day to live out your purpose to the glory of God. Finally, you can rest in knowing that no matter how imperfect you may feel as you grow in Christlikeness, nothing can change this one unshakable truth: you are a completely forgiven, fully accepted, deeply loved daughter of the King!

So let's choose now to love fearlessly from this day forward. Refuse to bow to fear, insecurity, or doubt anymore. Remember, you are perfectly loved, today and always. Then go teach your children to fear the Lord so that they, too, may know freedom in the perfect love of Christ.

Decide to not take life for granted, but to make your one life count. Do what ignites your soul in service of the kingdom of God and run your race with passion and purpose. Love others in a way that encourages them to keep running their race too. Walk humbly with Jesus all the days of your life, remembering as a member of the body of Christ you have become a part of a team that is strengthened, supported, and built up in the perfect love of God. Go ahead and say yes even when it's easier to say no. Take the risk. Your destiny awaits.

> They triumphed over him by the blood of the Lamb and by the word of their testimony; they did not love their lives so much as to shrink from death.
>
> —*Revelation* ***12:11***

STEP 12: LOVE FEARLESSLY

STUDY GUIDE

1. When you think about the different arenas of your life—relationships, schedule, work, finances, leisure activities, health, and so on—is there any arena in which you are not yet living perfectly loved? If so, what arena is that? What fears might still be lingering there?

2. 1 John 4:18 says, "There is no fear in love." How have the fears you listed above kept you from being able to love others freely and fearlessly? Will you pray and ask God to help you release all control to Him?

3. 1 John 4:19 says, "We love because he first loved us." Who has God called you to love, and how has He called you to love them? Pray and ask God to reveal three people whom you can choose to love fearlessly as Jesus has loved you. Write down practical ideas that come to mind next to each person's name. Then act on them!

4. Do you have a community of believers you do life with—not just a church you attend regularly, but also a group of godly friends who pour into you as you pour into them? How might you also be intentional about extending opportunities to other believers in need of community?

5. You were chosen by God for a special purpose: to "fearlessly make known the mystery of the gospel" (Ephesians 6:19). How can you be bold in sharing your faith with someone this week? Pray now, asking God for opportunities to share the gospel with boldness.

PRAYER:

Heavenly Father, Thank You for Your perfect love! This journey toward living perfectly loved has been challenging but also incredibly rewarding! Thank You for revealing Your plan for my rescue, restoration, and release. Teach me to love fearlessly and to live in unity with other believers in the body of Christ. Make me worthy of Your calling, Lord, and by Your power, bring to fruition my every desire for goodness and my every deed prompted by faith. In Jesus' name I pray, Amen.

AUTHOR'S NOTE: LIVING PERFECTLY LOVED

It's been 12 years since I sat at the bottom of that deep, dark pit of despair over my struggle with anxiety and fear. As I sit typing these words to you, reflecting on my journey from where it all began to *living perfectly loved,* tears of joy are flowing, and an overwhelming sense of victory fills my heart. Truly, God has been faithful to deliver me from my life of crippling anxiety and fear, to restore me, and now to release me to begin fearlessly loving and helping others. I'm in awe of the goodness of God and His overcoming power.

I have not yet "arrived," as I know it will take a lifetime to grow into Christlikeness and understand the depths of God's perfect love for me. I will need to continue to fight to stand firm in my freedom in Christ and call to mind these 12 steps I've learned, my 12 "stones of remembrance" (see Joshua 4:5–7). And yet I am confident in this: "I sought the LORD, and he answered me; he delivered me from all my fears" (Psalm 34:4). God has given me beauty for ashes, and I am now at peace with God and within myself. To God be the glory!

My prayer is that you too are now feeling this same freedom from the grip of anxiety and fear—or at very least are a few steps closer today than you were before starting this book. If you're feeling as though you're not yet where you would hope to be, please remember this faith journey is a marathon, not a sprint. Don't get discouraged if you've still got several steps yet to go. Instead, decide to keep moving forward one small step at a time. This could look like circling back to specific challenging chapters of this book to dig deeper with God into each one of the steps. Or, if you aren't yet involved in a small group at church or meeting regularly with a friend, pastor, or counselor, maybe it's finding your people—those you can connect with, whom you trust to love and support you as you continue on in your faith journey.

I would personally love to connect with you as well. You can reach out to me through my website at kellyannsnyder.com. It would be an honor to continue to support you in any way I can. Ultimately, my hope and prayer in vulnerably sharing my not-so-perfect journey from living in fear to living perfectly loved is that my testimony has encouraged you, better equipped you to overcome anxiety and fear, and inspired you to pursue God wholeheartedly and grow in your understanding of His perfect love for you. God bless you, friend!

ACKNOWLEDGMENTS

Thank You, God, for Your perfect love that casts out all my fear. I am forever grateful for Your amazing grace and patience with me. Thank You for giving me a passion, purpose, and the vision for writing this book, for entrusting me with its message, and for giving me the strength, wisdom, and support I needed to complete it. I give You all the glory!

To my husband, Todd. Thank you for praying for me and supporting me the whole way through my journey to living perfectly loved—from walking beside me through my personal pain, encouraging me through the writing process, funding the publication of this book, and everything in between. I would not have had the courage to persevere if not for you. From the bottom of my heart, thank you for loving me so well and for modeling for me how to love like Jesus. I love you with all my heart!

To my children, Riley and Janie. You are gifts from God. You light up my life with your enthusiasm, joy, creativity, love, and laughter. Thank you for the personal sacrifices you made that allowed me the time I needed to write for hours on end. Thank you for committing to pray for me and for cheering me on! It is my joy to love and serve you and to leave this book with you as a lasting legacy for generations to come.

To my family, friends, *Living Perfectly Loved* small group members, launch team, and all others who gathered around me to pray, offer insight and feedback, and champion my calling to write—I'm so grateful for your love and support. It takes the whole body of Christ. We are better together! Thank you from the bottom of my heart.

To Bethany McShurley who critiqued my first draft, thank you for widening my vision for this book. To Melissa Hogarty, my next developmental and copy editor, your intelligence, attention to detail, and insight will not be forgotten. You called every sentence into question and held me accountable for every word written before God. I learned so much from you about the craft of writing. Finally, to all those at Hope*Books, Brian Dixon, my inspiring cohort of fellow authors, and all who helped bring this book to publication, thank you for sharing my passion and vision for helping Christian women overcome anxiety and fear in the perfect love of God.

EMOTIONAL TRIGGERS LOG

Incident Date: ____________________

1. What happened?

____

____

2. Who were you with?

____

____

3. Where were you?

____

____

4. When did it occur (time/day)?

____

____

5. What physical symptoms did you experience (if any)?

____

____

6. How many times a day/week is this happening for you?

____

____

7. What thought(s) did you have just before the incident occurred?

____

____

8. What strong emotion(s) did you feel?

____

____

9. What painful past memory does this incident bring to mind?

____

____

10. What do your thoughts say about what you believe about God, others, and/or yourself?

____

____

11. If a painful memory was triggered—is there someone you can forgive, or a sin or attitude you can confess to God? Consider talking through this memory with a friend, pastor, or counselor who can help you reprocess and heal from the pain of your past. Ask God for His healing touch.

____

____

A GUIDE TO TAKING CAPTIVE EVERY THOUGHT: REPLACING WORN-OUT LIES WITH GOD'S TRUTH

Lie #1: Anxiety is just something I have to live with. It's a part of who I am.

Truth: "The thief comes only to steal and kill and destroy; I have come that they may have life, and have it to the full" (John 10:10).

Truth: "No, in all these things we are more than conquerors through him who loved us" (Romans 8:37).

Lie #2: I can't do this.

Truth: "I can do all this through him who gives me strength" (Philippians 4:13).

Truth: "Have I not commanded you? Be strong and courageous. Do not be afraid; do not be discouraged, for the LORD your God will be with you wherever you go" (Joshua 1:9).

Lie #3: I'm not enough.

Truth: "I praise you because I am fearfully and wonderfully made" (Psalm 139:14).

Truth: "His divine power has given us everything we need for a godly life through our knowledge of him who called us by his own glory and goodness" (2 Peter 1:3).

Lie #4: I'm not capable.

Truth: "Be strong and courageous, and do the work. Do not be afraid or discouraged, for the LORD God, my God, is with you. He will not fail you or forsake you until all the work for the service of the temple of the LORD is finished" (1 Chronicles 28:20).

Truth: "Being confident of this, that he who began a good work in you will carry it on to completion until the day of Christ Jesus" (Philippians 1:6).

Lie #5: I am unloved.

Truth: "I have loved you with an everlasting love; I have drawn you with unfailing kindness" (Jeremiah 31:3).

Truth: "As the Father has loved me, so have I loved you. Now remain in my love" (John 15:9).

Lie #6: I'm worthless. I am not worthy of love.

Truth: "Are not two sparrows sold for a penny? Yet not one of them will fall to the ground outside your Father's care. And even the very hairs of your head are all numbered. So don't be afraid; you are worth more than many sparrows" (Matthew 10:29–31).

Truth: "But God demonstrates his own love for us in this: While we were still sinners, Christ died for us" (Romans 5:8).

Lie #7: I'm all alone.

Truth: "So do not fear, for I am with you; do not be dismayed, for I am you God. I will strengthen you and help you; I will uphold you with my righteous right hand" (Isaiah 41:10).

Truth: "Never will I leave you; never will I forsake you" (Hebrews 13:5).

Lie #8: I need everyone to like me and think well of me.

Truth: "Am I now trying to win the approval of human beings, or of God? Or am I trying to please people? If I were still trying to please people, I would not be a servant of Christ" (Galatians 1:10).

Truth: "Fear of man will prove to be a snare, but whoever trusts in the LORD is kept safe" (Proverbs 29:25).

Lie #9: I have to be perfect to be worthy of love.

Truth: "For by one sacrifice he has made perfect forever those who are being made holy" (Hebrews 10:14).

Truth: "But now he has reconciled you by Christ's physical body through death to present you holy in his sight, without blemish and free from accusation" (Colossians 1:22).

Lie #10: If I put myself out there and open myself up, I'll just end up getting hurt.

Truth: "For whoever wants to save their life will lose it, but whoever loses their life for me will save it" (Luke 9:24).

Truth: "There is no fear in love. But perfect love drives out fear, because fear has to do with punishment. The one who fears is not made perfect in love. We love because he first loved us" (1 John 4:18–19).

Lie #11: I'm not good at relationships.

Truth: "You are the light of the world" (Matthew 5:14).

Truth: "It is God who works in you to will and to act in order to fulfill his good purpose" (Philippians 2:13).

Lie #12: What I say or do makes no difference. I have nothing to really offer anyone.

Truth: "But you are a chosen people, a royal priesthood, a holy nation, God's special possession, that you may declare the praises of him who called you out of darkness into his wonderful light" (1 Peter 2:9).

Truth: "Listen to me, you islands; hear this, you distant nations: Before I was born the LORD called me; from my mother's womb he has spoken my name" (Isaiah 49:1).

Lie #13: I've missed my calling. It's too late for me.

Truth: "For God's gifts and his call are irrevocable" (Romans 11:29).

Truth: "'For I know the plans I have for you,' declares the LORD, 'plans to prosper you and not to harm you, plans to give you hope and a future'" (Jeremiah 29:11).

Lie #14: I can't be forgiven. My past is unredeemable.

Truth: "Therefore, there is now no condemnation for those who are in Christ Jesus" (Romans 8:1).

Truth: "Therefore, my friends, I want you to know that through Jesus the forgiveness of sins is proclaimed to you. Through him everyone who believes is set free from every sin" (Acts 13:38–39).

Lie #15: I have to earn God's blessing and favor.

Truth: "Do not be afraid, little flock, for your Father has been pleased to give you the kingdom" (Luke 12:32).

Truth: "He who did not spare his own Son, but gave him up for us all—how will he not also, along with him, graciously give us all things?" (Romans 8:32)

Lie #16: If I let go of control, everything in my life will fall apart. I need to stay in control.

Truth: "Trust in the LORD with all your heart and lean not on your own understanding; in all your ways submit to him, and he will make your paths straight" (Proverbs 3:5–6).

Truth: "Come to me, all you who are weary and burdened, and I will give you rest. Take my yoke upon you and learn from me, for I am gentle and humble in heart, and you will find rest for your souls. For my yoke is easy and my burden is light" (Matthew 11:28–29).

Lie #17: I will never be free.

Truth: "So if the Son sets you free, you will be free indeed" (John 8:36).

Truth: "The One who breaks open the way will go up before them; they will break through the gate and go out. Their King will pass through before them, the LORD at their head" (Micah 2:13).

Lie #18: Bad things keep happening to me. I'm just one step away from my next crisis.

Truth: "They will have no fear of bad news; their hearts are steadfast, trusting in the LORD" (Psalm 112:7).

Truth: "Have no fear of sudden disaster or of the ruin that overtakes the wicked, for the LORD will be at your side and will keep your foot from being snared" (Proverbs 3:25–26).

Lie #19: There's no way out and no hope for me. My suffering is never going to end.

Truth: "And the God of all grace, who called you to his eternal glory in Christ, after you have suffered a little while, will himself restore you and make you strong, firm, and steadfast" (1 Peter 5:10).

Truth: "'For I know the plans I have for you,' declares the LORD, 'plans to prosper you and not to harm you, plans to give you hope and a future'" (Jeremiah 29:11).

Lie #20: I'm going to die.

Truth: "With long life I will satisfy him and show him my salvation" (Psalm 91:16).

Truth: "Since the children have flesh and blood, he too shared in their humanity so that by his death he might break the power of him who holds the power of death—that is, the devil—and free those who all their lives were held in slavery by their fear of death" (Hebrews 2:14–15).

Lie #21: My salvation is not secure.

Truth: "See, I have engraved you on the palms of my hands" (Isaiah 49:16).

Truth: "The one who is victorious will, like them, be dressed in white. I will never blot out the name of that person from the book of life, but will acknowledge that name before my Father and his angels" (Revelation 3:5).

A BIBLICAL GUIDE TO SPIRITUAL DELIVERANCE

REPENT

To repent means that the Holy Spirit has convicted you of your sin, and you are truly remorseful. It means that you can name your sin and have humbly accepted and admitted the truth—that you are in fact a sinner in need of the only one who can save you from your sins: Jesus Christ.

"In the past God overlooked such ignorance, but now he commands all people everywhere to repent" (Acts 17:30).

Coming into agreement with the spirit of fear and allowing fear to have authority over us *is sin we must repent of.* There may be other sins you need to repent of related to this. Pray and ask God to reveal these to you so you can be set free. Pride, idolatry, and unbelief are sins often closely associated with fear.

CONFESS

Once you have recognized your sin, you must take responsibility for it and confess it to your heavenly Father. Sin is not a result of your life circumstances or things done to you that were out of your control. To sin is a choice—no two ways about it. To confess means that you are ready to tell God what you did and ask for His forgiveness in the name of Jesus.

"If we confess our sins, he is faithful and just and will forgive us our sins and purify us from all unrighteousness" (1 John 1:9).

You can pray in your own words or use the following scripted prayer to confess to God your sin: *Heavenly Father, I confess to You my sin of_____, which You have revealed to me through the conviction of the Holy Spirit. I repent of coming into agreement with the lies fear has spoken to me, for not believing and trusting in You wholeheartedly, and for _____. I take full responsibility for it all now. I ask You to forgive me and to release me from the power of this sin over my life. Father, cover me with the blood of Jesus. In the mighty name of Jesus I pray, Amen!*

RENOUNCE

This is where many believers stop. They confess their sins and ask for forgiveness, but they fail to formally turn away from their sin. In other words, we need to love ourselves but hate our sin. Google defines *renounce* as to "declare that one will no longer engage in or support." By renouncing your sin, you are making a declaration that you will no longer continue in this sin, and you are choosing to turn away from it.

"Renounce your sins by doing what is right, and your wickedness by being kind to the oppressed. It may be that then your prosperity will continue" (Daniel 4:27).

You can renounce your sin in your own words or by declaring the following out loud: *Spirit of fear (and/or unbelief, pride, idolatry, etc.), I renounce you and everything you stand for in my life. I will no longer serve you. I take a stand against you in Jesus' name. I will discern you and help others discern you all the days of my life.*

DRIVE OUT

If you have deep-rooted sin in your life, you may be experiencing demonic oppression. If you are a Christian, that does not mean you are demon-possessed, but perhaps that you have some evil spirits hanging around you, influencing your thoughts and behavior. They harass, afflict, and weigh you down. In order to be set free from ongoing demonic oppression, you may need to take this next step and effectively remove the evil spirit(s) from your life. Jesus has given you the authority as His disciple to drive out demons, and this includes any that want to harass you.

"As you go, proclaim this message: 'The kingdom of heaven has come near.' Heal the sick, raise the dead, cleanse those who have leprosy, drive out demons. Freely you have received; freely give" (Matthew 10:7–8).

When you are ready and have completed the previous steps, declare the truth out loud in your own words or speak the following: *Spirit of fear (or other), I have repented before my Father in heaven for serving you and allowing you control. By the power and authority of Jesus Christ in me, and by His blood that covers me, you must leave me now and go where Jesus tells you to go.*

Now breathe. If you need to, you can pray this prayer again and again. If you are taking authority in Christ over multiple spirits, I suggest you do it one at a time. Then, like David, you can victoriously declare, "I sought the Lord, and he answered me; he delivered me from all my fears" (Psalm 34:4).

GIVE THANKS

Embrace your newfound freedom and give thanks to God for His deliverance! It is finished! The blood of Jesus is your victory! The weight of your sin was nailed to the cross with Jesus, and you are completely forgiven! If you took the extra step to drive out demonic oppression and are now free from it, you will know. You may feel like a tremendous weight has been lifted or like you had been holding your breath for a long time and can finally breathe deeply. You will be overwhelmed with thanksgiving and gratitude for the deliverance God has brought you.

"He brought them out of darkness, the utter darkness, and broke away their chains. Let them give thanks to the LORD for his unfailing love and his wonderful deeds for mankind" (Psalm 107:14–15).

You can use your own words or use the following scripted prayer to give thanks: *Thank You, Father, for Your forgiveness! Thank You for Your peace, freedom, and unconditional love. Jesus, thank You for Your faithfulness to deliver me and Your promise to see me through to victory! You are worthy, my Lord and Savior, of all my worship and praise!*

RESIST

After experiencing deliverance from demonic oppression, you must make yourself ready for the possible backlash, or spiritual attack, that is likely to come soon after. God's Word tells us how to be prepared for this.

"Therefore put on the full armor of God, so that when the day of evil comes, you may be able to stand your ground, and after you have done everything, to stand" (Ephesians 6:13).

The enemy will attempt to remind you of your failure or even try to convince you that the breakthrough you experienced never really happened. He does not want you to stay free. He may try to downplay your experience, as if it could be explained away by coincidence or a change in your personal circumstances, rather than the power of Jesus that set you free.

You may be tempted to believe that you are still bound and return to the same sin. The enemy may try to create confusion or doubt in your mind to deceive you and to strip you of the testimony you now carry in Christ Jesus, leaving you feeling empty-handed. He will use any matter of influence or area of weakness he can to cause you to stumble and fall back into your old ways. I remember hearing the enemy whispering his lies in my ear—*Who said you were free? You will never be free.* Resist the enemy when he tries to come back. Fill yourself up with the Word of God. Don't leave any space vacant for the enemy to potentially manipulate his way back into your life.

"When an impure spirit comes out of a person, it goes through arid places seeking rest and does not find it. Then it says, 'I will return to the house I left.' When it arrives, it finds the house swept clean and put in order. Then it goes and takes seven other spirits more wicked than itself, and they go in and live there. And the final condition of that person is worse than the first" (Luke 11:24–26).

"Submit yourselves, then, to God. Resist the devil, and he will flee from you" (James 4:7).

By continuing to humbly submit yourself to God in true repentance, the Holy Spirit will empower you to resist the devil, and he and his demons will leave you. The sanctification process is ongoing, but oppression doesn't have to be. No matter what—if fear, unbelief, hopelessness, defeat, or anything else starts trying to creep back into your life—this is the work of the enemy! Look to the Word of God that speaks truth over you and empowers you—and take your stand against the devil's schemes.

"It is for freedom that Christ has set us free. Stand firm, then, and do not let yourselves be burdened again by a yoke of slavery" (Galatians 5:1).

PROCLAIM THE GOOD NEWS

Now you can be used by God to help set others free. You can share your testimony of how Jesus Christ delivered and saved you—and in doing so, God will not only set others free through you, but He will "repay you for the years the locusts have eaten" (Joel 2:25). He will redeem your story and give you a ministry through which He can be glorified!

"The Spirit of the Sovereign LORD is on me, because the LORD has anointed me to proclaim good news to the poor. He has sent me to bind up the brokenhearted, to proclaim freedom for the captives and release from darkness for the prisoners" (Isaiah 61:1).

SMALL GROUP LEADER'S GUIDE

Do you have a women's small group, book club, or group of friends with whom you'd like to work through this book? If so, you might consider using this leader's guide, which includes a sample timeline with the book content to cover each week, a sample lesson plan outline for how you might run each group meeting, and discussion questions. I've personally used this plan to lead several of my Living Perfectly Loved small groups through the 12 steps detailed in this book. This guide will help you feel confident in leading your small group, and it will help the women who attend feel comfortable, inspired, encouraged, equipped, and cared about. Finally, keep in mind that this is only a guide. You know your group and their needs best. Therefore, feel free to make adjustments as you see fit.

LOGISTICS

I have found weekly meetings to be most beneficial for groups I've led; ideally, plan for your group to meet weekly for 13 weeks. If you need to schedule meetings every other week, that could also work. Another suggestion would be to break up the content into parts. For example, you could work through part one as a group in the fall, break through the holiday season, and then pick back up in the spring with parts two and three. However you decide to approach the material with your group, I strongly recommend that you cover the content from only one chapter each meeting. Otherwise, the content might start to feel overwhelming, making it hard for group members to focus on taking just one small step at a time in their journey to *living perfectly loved*.

Should you have any further questions about leading your small group using this study, if you're looking for additional resources for your group members, or if you simply want to share with me how your group is responding to the book, I'd love to hear from you! Please contact me through my website (kellyannsnyder.com) or email me at kelly@kellyannsnyder.com, and I will get back to you.

TIMELINE

WEEK 1: Introduction: The Father's Love

WEEK 2: Step 1: Call Upon the Lord for Help

WEEK 3: Step 2: Uncover Emotional Triggers by Excavating Your Past

WEEK 4: Step 3: Take Captive Every Thought: Fear Is a Liar

WEEK 5: Step 4: Surrender Your Life and Live for Christ

WEEK 6: Step 5: Believe—Jesus Is Your Chain Breaker

WEEK 7: Step 6: Experience Perfect Peace in God's Presence

WEEK 8: Step 7: Rebuild Your Identity and Secure Your Faith in Christ

WEEK 9: Step 8: Prepare for Promotion: Stand Firm through the Testing of Your Faith

WEEK 10: Step 9: Let Go of Your Past and Embrace Your Purpose Today

WEEK 11: Step 10: Let Your Light Shine by Helping Others

WEEK 12: Step 11: Renew Your Strength in the Lord

WEEK 13: Step 12: Love Fearlessly and Author's Note: Living Perfectly Loved

---

LESSON PLAN OUTLINE

WELCOME (5 minutes)

- Greet each person and welcome any newcomers to the group.
- Have a sign in sheet ready with a space for everyone's name, email, and phone number. Always get permission before sharing contact information within the group and use contact information appropriately (i.e. not for forwards, spam emails, peer-to-peer marketing, etc.).
- Allow a few minutes for small talk and for everyone to settle in.

OPEN IN PRAYER (1–2 minutes)

- Be sure to pray before the start of each group meeting. You can open in prayer as the group leader, or ask for a volunteer to open in prayer. I always pray to invite God's presence and for conversation to flow naturally and to move where the Holy Spirit directs.

ICE BREAKER QUESTION (10 minutes)

- Ask each group member to share (if they feel comfortable): What is one "trigger" and one "glimmer" you experienced this week? By *trigger,* I mean a time they felt anxiety and fear provoke or grip them, and by *glimmer,* I mean something they experienced or did this week that helped them feel more at peace and joy-filled.

CHAPTER REVIEW AND DISCUSSION (25–30 minutes)

- Review the questions presented in the study guide at the end of each chapter, and choose a few to discuss as a group. Note: some questions will be ideal for group discussion, while others may be best kept for a time of personal reflection.
- In addition to reviewing some, or all, of the study guide questions specific to each step, you can ask these questions each week . . .
    1. What is one sentence or section of the chapter you highlighted, and why?
    2. What is one breakthrough idea shared in this chapter that shifted your mindset or changed your perspective?
    3. What one Scripture reference especially encouraged you or challenged you?
    4. What was your biggest overall takeaway from this chapter?
    5. What practical piece of advice did you take away from this chapter that you can begin implementing right away?
    6. What is God speaking to your heart about this week?

CLOSE IN PRAYER (10 minutes)

- It's important for your group members to know they are being prayed for each week, and for you to encourage them to share their prayer requests with the group. There are many ways to go about this. One way is to allow each person to verbalize their prayer requests and for the group to pray on the spot for each request. Depending on the size of your group this could take a significant amount of time. If your time is limited, you might prefer to pass around a sheet of paper or cards for everyone to write down their prayer requests on during your group time. Then, within 24 hours you can email those requests out to the whole group to be praying for throughout the week. Whatever approach you decide on, I encourage you to close out your group time with one final prayer, either led by you or a member of your group.

ANNOUNCEMENTS (1–2 minutes)

> Share with your group any information you have about upcoming church events, social gatherings, and service projects. Consider offering the group opportunities to participate in these events together.

BIBLIOGRAPHY

American Psychological Association Dictionary of Psychology. s.v. "Automatic Thoughts." Accessed September 4, 2023. https://dictionary.apa.org/automatic-thoughts.

American Psychological Association Dictionary of Psychology. s.v. "Fight-or-Flight Response." Accessed September 4, 2023. https://dictionary.apa.org/fight-or-flight-response.

Anxiety & Depression Association of America. "Chronic Pain." *Understand Anxiety and Depression* (blog), accessed September 4, 2023. www.adaa.org/understanding-anxiety/related-illnesses/other-related-conditions/chronic-pain.

Anxiety & Depression Association of America. "Did You Know?" *Understand Anxiety and Depression* (blog), accessed September 4, 2023. www.adaa.org/understanding-anxiety/facts-statistics.

Batterson, Mark. *Soulprint*. Colorado Springs, CO: Multnomah Books, 2011.

Carver, Jeff. "Spiritual Gifts Test." Spiritual Gifts Test. Accessed September 4, 2023. https://www.spiritualgiftstest.com.

Ciuciu, Asheritah. "The Ultimate Guide to Connect with God." *Creative Devos* (blog). *One Thing Alone Ministries*, accessed September 4, 2023. www.onethingalone.com/ultimate-list-creative-ways-connect-god-120-ideas/.

Dr. Seuss. *Oh, the Places You'll Go!* New York, NY: Random House Children's Books, 1990.

Goldfarb, Robyn. "Breaking Free from a Poverty Mindset," Wealth of Geeks. March 5, 2021. https://wealthofgeeks.com/poverty-mindset/. Accessed January 24, 2024.

Greenberger, Dennis and Christine A. Padesky. *Mind Over Mood.* New York, NY: The Guilford Press, 1995.

Harvard Health Publishing. "Pain, Anxiety, and Depression." *Mind & Mood* (blog). *Harvard Medical School*, September 16, 2021. www.health.harvard.edu/mind-and-mood/pain-anxiety-and-depression. Accessed January 24, 2024.

Idleman, Kyle. *Not a Fan*. Grand Rapids, MI: Zondervan, 2011.

It's a Wonderful Life. Dir. Frank Capra. Perf. James Stewart, Donna Reed, Lionel Barrymore, and Thomas Mitchell. RKO, 1946. Film.

Jerusalem Prayer Team. "The Oil of Unity." Accessed September 4, 2023. https://www.jerusalemprayerteam.org/2017/07/31/the-oil-of-unity/.

King, Dr. Martin Luther, Jr. "'Loving Your Enemies,' Sermon Delivered at Dexter Avenue Baptist Church." November 17, 1957, *King Papers* (blog). *Stanford: The Martin Luther King, Jr. Research and Education Institute,* accessed September 4, 2023. https://kinginstitute.stanford.edu/king-papers/documents/loving-your-enemies-sermon-delivered-dexter-avenue-baptist-church.

Leonard, Jayne. "What Does Anxiety Feel Like and How Does It Affect the Body?" Medical News Today. Updated May 26, 2023. https://www.medicalnewstoday.com/articles/322510.

Meeker, Craig. "The Monarchs." Steps to Life. February 6, 2020. www.stepstolife.org/article/the-monarchs/. Accessed September 4, 2023

Moore, Beth (@bethmoorelmp). "Our God-ordained callings have never been..." Instagram post, February 7, 2019. www.instagram.com/p/BtlULvKgCI-/. Accessed September 4, 2023.

Nouwen, Henri. *Making All Things New*. San Francisco, CA: HarperOne, 2009.

Olsen, Ted. "The Real St. Patrick." *Christian History* (blog). *Christianity Today*, accessed June 24, 2023. www.christianitytoday.com/history/2008/august/real-st-patrick.html.

Parke, Blair. "Yeshua: Deliverer, Savior – Why This Name of God Is So Important for Today." Bible Study Tools. November 23, 2019. www.biblestudytools.com/bible-study/topical-studies/yeshua-deliverer-savior.html. Accessed September 4, 2023.

Rebecca. "St. Patrick's Breastplate. A Shield for Divine Protection." *News* (blog), *Columban* Sisters, accessed September 4, 2023. www.columbansisters.org/st-patricks-breastplate-a-shield-for-divine-protection/.

Right Now Media. www.rightnowmedia.org.

Shirer, Priscilla. *Armor of God.* Nashville, TN: Lifeway Press, 2022.

Tomlin, Chris. "Whom Shall I Fear (God of Angel Armies)." Track 3 on *Burning Lights,* released November 9, 2012. Sixsteps.

Voskamp, Ann. *One Thousand Gifts.* Grand Rapids, MI: Zondervan, 2010.

Wallnau, Lance. "When God shows you a vision, a passion, a picture..." Facebook post, October 24, 2020. www.facebook.com/LanceWallnau/posts/10158888593284936. Accessed September 4, 2023.

Williams, Zach. "Chain Breaker." Track 1 on *Chain Breaker*, released December 14, 2016. Essential Records.

CONNECT WITH KELLY

Kelly Ann Snyder is a Christian writer, speaker, and teacher passionate about helping others live free from fear and full of joy, secure in God's perfect love. Grateful to God for rescuing her from fear, she started a blog and a podcast, launched a small group for women at her church, and wrote her first book, Living Perfectly Loved. With a B.A. in Communication and a teaching credential, Kelly served as a public school educator for 17 years. Kelly enjoys fresh flowers, nature walks, decorating, sipping tea, and studying God's Word. She lives in sunny San Diego, California with her loving husband and two teenage children. Discover more ways to connect with Kelly at KELLYANNSNYDER.COM

Printed in the USA
CPSIA information can be obtained
at www.ICGtesting.com
LVHW091331300524
781622LV00006B/6